*Corpus in Extremis* is an extraordinary story of survival and resilience against considerable challenges centred around Smith's brittle bones. Despite all, she tells her memoir with vigour and good humour taking the 'dis' out of disability and wiping the floor with it.

—Sara Hardy, author of *The Unusual Life of Edna Walling* and *A Secretive Life*

This exquisitely written memoir tells compelling tales about broken bones and heartbreak, as well as about one extraordinary woman's strong-willed and creative mind and quiet courage. While Smith navigates difficulties unimaginable to most of us in her everyday, she's woven out of their painful threads such a vital story of a passionately lived life that I found it difficult to part with the book when it came to an end.

—Lee Kofman, author of *The Writer Laid Bare* and *Imperfect*

LORETTA SMITH is a Melbourne-based writer. Her bestselling biography *A Spanner in the Works: The extraordinary story of Alice Anderson and Australia's first 'all-girl' garage* (Hachette, 2019) has been optioned for a TV series and inspired the play, *Garage Girls,* performed to a sell-out audience at La Mama Theatre in 2023. The play toured regionally throughout Victoria in 2024 as part of the VCE playlist. *Corpus in Extremis: A Memoir* is her second book.

Other books by Loretta Smith

*A Spanner in the Works: The Extraordinary Story of Alice Anderson and Australia's First 'All-Girl' Garage* (2019)

# CORPUS IN EXTREMIS

## A Memoir

Loretta Smith

We respectfully acknowledge the wisdom of Aboriginal and Torres Strait
Islander peoples and their custodianship of the lands and waterways.
The Countries on which Spinifex offices are situated are Djuru, Bunurong
and Wurundjeri, Wadawurrung, Gundungarra and Noongar.

First published by Spinifex Press, 2024

Spinifex Press Pty Ltd
PO Box 200, Little River, VIC 3211, Australia
PO Box 105, Mission Beach, QLD 4852, Australia

women@spinifexpress.com.au
www.spinifexpress.com.au

Edited by Susan Hawthorne and Pauline Hopkins
Cover design by Deb Snibson
Typesetting by Helen Christie, Blue Wren Books
Typeset in Arno
Printed in the USA

A catalogue record for this
book is available from the
National Library of Australia

NATIONAL LIBRARY OF AUSTRALIA

ISBN: 9781922964069 (paperback)
ISBN: 9781922964076 (ebook)

For my family

*Was I related to the three-thousand-year-old Egyptian mummy, a child with thin, fractured bones and heart-shaped skull on display in the British Museum? Or perhaps 'Ivar the Boneless', the prince from ninth-century Denmark who was unable to walk on his soft legs and was, as legend has it, carried into battle on a shield? In an earlier time and place I would have been cast out, left in the forest for the wolves to devour.*

*My past is a question mark, my future an experiment.*

Author's note: Some names in this book have been changed to protect the privacy of the individuals.

# CONTENTS

# LIFE IS A BOX MARKED 'FRAGILE'
## (And I may as well be made of cardboard)

### Bloodlines—mother

My mother Lyn-don't-ever-call-me-Lynette Smith née Little, was short and petite with curly brown hair and large blue-grey eyes. She had high expectations for herself and her family. We were meant to be the picture-perfect version from which she could escape her own childhood. The stories from her past were often laced with cruelty and disappointment—or at least that's my recollection because those were the stories filled with tension and drama. Mum learned to swim by being thrown from her father's shoulders into the deep end of the local creek and, by her account, almost drowning. Mum never got to go to high school and the nuns, who ran her Catholic primary school, controlled their charges by threatening to lock them in the 'black hole'— a place under the platform in the assembly hall.

If Mum didn't end up in the black hole for some minor misdemeanour, she was boxed around the ears for daydreaming in class. The middle child of seven, she'd often felt invisible, as if there were moments people forgot she existed. When she later discovered she was hearing-impaired, I wondered if it was from the numerous childhood ear infections and the reason she was boxed round the ears for daydreaming. 'Just a minute, I can't hear without my glasses!' she often said. Maybe she felt invisible because her eyes were tired and she couldn't hear everything the world had to say.

She walked with her siblings to early-morning mass every day before school. Sometimes it was so cold the ground was white with frost and her bare legs ached. On Sundays the whole family went to church dressed in their finest, the outfits designed and made by their father, the tailor. There was never much money but on Sundays they looked a million pounds, the pressures of home life hidden in their pockets. The church aisle was their catwalk. For Mum, church felt safer and more promising than family or school. She took to praying a lot.

We must have gone to church on my thirteenth birthday, being a Sunday. It was rare for us to miss the weekly sermon. People at church must have wished me happy birthday. Was there a cake? I think there was a cake. I recall my mother smiling but seeming sad, distant, even a little distressed.

My body hadn't registered adolescence in the least: no sprouting of hair, pimples, breasts, nothing. I was as dormant as our winter garden, bare-limbed and bud-less. Mum said once you become a teenager the hormones kick in and all sorts of changes occur, including acting strange and moody. But the only person acting strange on my thirteenth birthday was my mother.

I didn't want anything to be wrong on my thirteenth birthday.

I didn't know how to ask her what might be wrong.

I didn't want to be the thing that was wrong.

Mum had told me that every time I cried at night Dad would hit the roof. Mum had never seen this side to him. He was a mild-mannered gentleman. He was the one she'd committed the rest of her life to. Dreams of perfect family bliss fell away as dread rained down on her Catholic head. Catholic guilt pressed at the back of my own eyes and weighed down my limbs when Mum first told me this. Dad was very anxious, and it seemed I was the main cause.

One evening Mum cried out, 'I want to be ME!'

Mum's frustrations morphed into projects of creativity. She planted pampas grass, wrote poetry, came home with vases from pottery class and macrame to make hanging baskets and, as a child, she dressed me like a fancy doll, with outfits more like costumes than day wear. I had hats and capes, and things with satin and velvet ribbons. I dressed in velvet pants with socks pulled up to my knees in emulation of Sebastian Bear from the *Magic Circle Club* children's television show. I was a spy, a racing driver, I could run and play and dance and be anything I wanted to be. I could dress like the little girl in *Chitty Chitty Bang Bang*.

What did I wear on my thirteenth birthday? Was it the maxi-dress Mum had made with the puffed sleeves and shirred bodice? I thought I looked so glamorous, especially when I got gold sandals to match. Or was this the day I wore my favourite bright multi-coloured suede shoes and new jeans? If it was, I remember standing in the rumpus room in a shaft of sunlight. I wasn't aware I had my toes turned inwards until Dad walked past and told me to straighten my feet. He told me I looked retarded standing like that. Sad clown feet, a patchwork of yellow, blue and red laughing in the sun. Point toe straight or outward, never in.

Late in the afternoon of my thirteenth birthday Mum disappeared. I eventually found her on the back steps, an Alpine cigarette between her fingers. I stood in the doorframe and looked at my feet. She turned round. Her eyes were red from crying.

'The doctors said you wouldn't live long enough to become a teenager. And look at you! A miracle.' She butted her cigarette out and stood up. 'The doctors didn't know what they were talking about!'

I didn't know, either.

## Bloodlines—father

Summer holidays 1983. My friend and I took advantage of the university break and drove north along the coast, feeding my little hatchback with leaded petrol at forty cents a litre. On a nude beach in Noosa we communed with the moon-tides, water in our hearts, our kidneys, our lungs and brains. Even bones are watery.

The phone call arrived at the reception desk of a Sydney youth hostel. The message: phone home.

The receptionist expected us to go to a public phone box to return the call. Did I have the right coins? My hands couldn't find the slot. The handset was filthy and dead. I only knew I was still gathered inside my flesh because I could hear my breath, fast and shallow. I returned to reception and begged to make a short call to Melbourne. They could add it to the bill. Mum got on the line. 'Your father died this morning.'

He was fifty-three years old.

The last time we'd spoken it was an argument over something so trivial I couldn't recall.

We headed for the Hume, an ugly highway but more direct than the coastal route. Solid objects shimmered and wilted. I wound down the window, willing myself to breathe. We pulled into the servo. I took the toilet key attached to a block of wood from the attendant and locked the filthy door behind me.

It was dark and the mirror reflected only the whites of my eyes. I didn't turn on the light. I didn't want the light to know I was here. I adjusted to the gloom and stared back at the face in front of me. I brought a hand to my cheek. Who made my face? How much of him is carried in me? What has he left behind? In the mirror I saw his curly hair, though mine is browner, his greying black. I saw his olive skin. I looked at my thumbs. They are his in miniature. I look at my thonged feet. They are the same as his, thin and pointy-toed.

He used to take me out on the wet sand and we'd jog in bare feet to help strengthen my loose tendons. He bought me my first runners, even though I couldn't run. They were pale blue Adidas ones with navy stripes. Once, he took me into the waves on his back. I wrapped my arms around his neck and rested my chin between his shifting shoulder blades as he swam to the sandbank. A shark siren pierced the sky. I let go and swam back before he had time to turn. My arms have always served me better than my legs.

In full light, the whites of my eyes were a pale egg-blue, an indication of my 1 in 20,000 genetic anomaly. My eyes are large like my mother's but they are hazel, a mixture of my father's brown and my mother's blue. I blended into the dark, feeling this moment against everything that has been and everything that is to come. My father was dead and one day I will be dead too. If I am lucky my face will be given enough time to age.

On the morning before his death, my father picked Mum's favourite rose from the garden and handed it to her. Around 3 a.m. Mum woke to find Dad breathing noisily. She nudged him, he rolled to the floor, unconscious. My brother attempted resuscitation. He was still breathing when the ambulance came but died en route to hospital. My family was told it was better that he'd gone. Had he lived, his body would have been merely a shell; an empty seashell except for the sound of wind and waves, tiding time.

There was a knock on the door. I splashed my face with water and turned the knob. The elderly woman looked friendly enough, but I immediately resented her for no reason other than she'd managed to outlive my father.

We'd taken three weeks to meander up the eastern seaboard. We took two days to return. I took over the driving. On a curve I hit dry sand, veered to the opposite side of the road and crashed into a wire fence. No damage, just grief, then laughter at cheating the beast. A moment sooner or later and we'd have been collected by a prime mover.

Who was my father? He rarely spoke of his past. We gleaned a little from black and white photographs and stories Mum regaled us with secondhand. A barefoot, tanned child living in rundown rentals on the outskirts of Brisbane. An overbearing mother, with my father's dark handsome features. His father, a pale, overweight station master with sandy blonde hair, long dead. A brother with club feet who never left home. A sister who married an alcoholic. A work transfer to Melbourne where he escaped and met my mother.

My father was an anxious man made all the more anxious by me, his firstborn, with a rare bone condition the doctors said would not see me live to my teens; watery bones that bent and twisted and broke. He loved us but didn't know how to relate to us. Little ones were noisy, unpredictable. Five was too many. He worried about money and the weight of responsibility. He worked as a customs agent for the same company for twenty-five years but never received a gold watch. On Saturdays he caught up with neighbours and washed the company car. On Sundays he came to church and gave us twenty cents for the plate—never more, never less—even though he was Protestant, not Catholic, and couldn't take communion.

I have his childhood tin box of treasures with Keep Out scratched in large, awkward letters on the lid. Inside, there are old coins, a few knucklebones, feathers and a roll of cash. The notes are from World War Two and made by the Japanese as victory currency before they bombed Darwin. Proof of thwarted ambition.

My father, Harold-don't-ever-call-him-Harry is already in the morgue and I try to square that with the last time I saw him. The big full stop. Until now I'd only lived with commas.

Mum refused an autopsy. What did it matter when nothing would bring him back? And we reckoned we'd worked it out ourselves. Three months earlier he'd jacked up my ancient Mini Minor to work on it. He was under the car when the jack collapsed. His calf became swollen and he decided to bandage his leg. We think a blood clot formed, a blood clot that took three months to reach his heart.

I don't remember the funeral except that I wore an outfit my mother had made that my father had said was his favourite. At the cemetery the grave smelled like our yard after Dad had mown the grass. As the coffin was lowered, Mum whispered, 'Bye-bye Hal.' His headstone lists all our names as if we are buried with him.

I still feel the weight of my old car on him.


## I am a rare specimen

1961. A hug. A cracked rib. A cry. A hug. A cracked rib. How many cracks? How could anyone know that every time I was handled it caused me pain? It was before I understood words. I was a baby who learned to cry less, not more. My instinct drew me to stillness, shallow breath, hushed lungs.

It was six months before I gave any outward sign that something was peculiarly different. It was inadvertent. I stood, gripping the wooden rails of my cot, left foot flat, right foot raised. My mother was concerned enough to take me to the doctor but he merely patted her on the arm, told her first-time mothers were all the same, worrying too much. There was nothing wrong. I was a perfectly normal-looking baby he said.

The truth, hidden beneath skin and muscle, was eventually prised open when I fell out of my highchair aged twelve months. I didn't cry, just slumped like a rag doll with a white-as-porcelain head, broken and floating in cerebral fluid.

X-rays charted my insides. Against a vertical plate, my mother's enormous skeletal hands held me between my tiny ribs, each shadowy image throwing up multiple fractures, probably one for every time I'd been cradled. So many healed and healing bones. When the specialist momentarily left the room, my mother whipped his notes round and saw *abuse?* scrawled there.

What was wrong? The doctors mulled while a young trainee nurse visited the children's ward after attending a lecture on hip dysplasia. She checked every infant's groin and there I was with my bandaged head. My hip sockets, which should have been worn into even, bilateral grooves by continuous movement of my infant legs were out of whack. My broken skull had brought me here but the doctors had failed to appreciate the top storey was merely an indication of faulty foundations. If I were a building you would want to raze me to the ground and start again.

If it were hip dysplasia alone, I would have been the one-in-six-hundred-baby-girls statistic. But the bone fractures, the slightly blue sclera of my eyes and the overly flexible joints put me in that 1-in-20,000 category that carried the name Osteogenesis Imperfecta (OI). Bones-imperfect-from-the-beginning. I wasn't being thrown against a wall or pushed from a highchair. I had brittle bones caused by a collagen defect. I was a rare specimen but also a conundrum according to the doctors in those early years of the 1960s. My condition should have been more pronounced. Where was the heart-shaped head? The truncated torso? The barrel chest? The shortened limbs? OI sub-groups were yet to be defined, the mapping of the human genome decades away. I was labelled a syndrome, the patterns of a disorder for which I was not quite fitting the full category. Just as Willem Vrolik, the nineteenth-century Dutch anatomist who first observed the condition and described its various aspects as Vrolik Syndrome, I required a more accurate signifier.

Did I inherit it from my mother or father? Both displayed hyper-laxity in the way they leaned back into their knee joints and my mother was diagnosed with a hearing impairment in her thirties, sometimes a sign of OI. It could have come from either parent but more than likely it was that random mix of one or more recessive genes drawn from each chromosomal pond, though there was—and still is—no cure. OI, I have been told, is a complicated, hydra-headed genetic beast.

X-ray after X-ray on my fragile frame. This angle, that angle, legs up down and sideways. Each time the technician covered me with a large protective lead apron and laid two pennies where he hoped my ovaries were. Beneath the weight I was hardly visible but central to the activity. I understood they were taking photos of my insides but I sensed the rest in the way an animal senses fear, in the lead pinning me down, in the sights of a bright flash from which everyone fled.

The X-rays piled up, a giant family album of skeletons. My father arrived in his business suit and demanded the doctors tell him exactly how many X-rays had been taken. A tally was done and the doctors blanched. At three years old I had absorbed the radiation of over four hundred of them, often taken repeatedly over the same body parts. I didn't suffer the long exposure burn marks and hair loss of the earliest X-ray patients of the late nineteenth century but medical imaging in the 1960s nevertheless took longer and delivered a dangerous radiation load compared to today's millisecond image capture. Radiation exposure is cumulative, which is why I was covered in a lead apron and copper pennies to protect me from cancer and sterility. My body was showcased time and again but no one working in the complicated cogs of the hospital system thought to check that the X-rays they requested had duplicate copies. Multiple duplicate copies. And like the 'X' in X-ray—first coined in 1895 as an 'unknown phenomenon' by German physicist Wilhelm Conrad Roentgen after radiating his wife's hand to reveal the image of her bones beneath—my condition was little understood and my future experimental.

# THE ADULTS ARE IN CHARGE

## (But not always incommunicado)

**The infancy of infant pain: don't give a child opioids, oh no**

1964. I swing my head back and forth in my metal hospital cot singing 'baa baa back shee hav oo any woo' and it shifts the pain threshold. The world spins and the rhythm sends me swimming elsewhere. Anywhere. Everywhere but where it hurts. Swish, swish back and forth. Until I am stopped by a nurse for disturbing the other children.

But it wasn't me who disturbed Jillie in the other ward. She cried on and on no matter what any nurse or doctor seemed to do. Jillie had plaster over her legs too. 'Baa baa back shee' helped me stop Jillie's crying in my ears. The louder she cried the louder I sang and swished. When I stopped the world became deliciously dizzy. And it was then that Jillie sometimes stopped too. I could sink into my dizziness just for a quiet moment. Then she would start again. I imagined great big sobs wet her pillow.

I don't recall ever being administered pain relief in hospital or at home as a young child. At the time there was still a general belief among the medical profession that children did not feel pain, that their central nervous system is not developed enough. This belief was based on a combination of ignorance and the twin fear of addiction and respiratory depression in children. In the early 1960s, opioids were commonly administered to adults in hospitals but used very sparingly with children. And they were administered in such low doses they weren't effective. In fact, major paediatric textbooks of the 1950s rarely mention pain. Not until the 1980s was there an 'overdue recognition that newborns and other children could indeed experience severe pain which was often poorly managed … [and that] Unrelieved, severe pain is not only cruel but life-threatening.'

The colourful history of opioid use across the world and in particular in Australia may well have led to the practice of avoiding the treatment of paediatric pain. In colonial Australia opioids were unregulated and widely used. Salesmen, chemists and milk bars did a roaring trade in their 'soothing syrups' available in liquid, powder or lozenges catering to all ages, even infants under six months. Apart from being popular as an anti-diarrhoea medication at a time when diarrhoea was responsible for half of infant deaths, opioid medications were widely advertised as a remedy for cough, teething and colic. In 1903, the Surgeon Superintendent of New South Wales, Dr Philip Muskett wrote in *The Illustrated Australian Medical Guide* of the great benefits of opioids in treating sick children. He promoted using chlorodyne (a morphine-based mixture) as indispensable in every household. Dr Muskett advised the use of such medicine for a vast array of paediatric maladies from herpes zoster to night terrors. But the harm soon became apparent as infant deaths from such medications overrode deaths from diarrhoea and laws were finally introduced to restrict 'soothing syrups.'

The only soothing syrup I had access to was the self-administered kind of rocking back and forth and singing. And the only things I knew that didn't feel pain were dolls and teddy bears because they didn't have real insides. They didn't even have bones.

The nurse again told me to stop my singing and swishing, her brows in a knot, her eyes filled with consternation I took as disapproval. When Jillie's crying again bounced off the walls and up the corridor, she would take in a sharp breath and move off, her rubber-soled shoes squeaking on the linoleum like frightened mice.

When Jillie's plaster was finally removed with the giant metal scissors, it was there for all to see—a plaster torment. An invisible dent in the first layers of plaster, an undetected air pocket, a hole so deep into Jillie's foot the doctors and nurses could see the bone. I never set eyes on Jillie but it was a nurse who told me why the wailing had ceased.

I tried to imagine what that sort of pain would have felt like. I knew from two years of age that every pain had its own language. But I couldn't think on it for very long because I imagined that sort of pain too well, the worrying of the plaster indent with every move, pushing its way into her tender foot.

Such knowledge made my world unsteady. In a place away from my parents, with starched grown-ups, beeping machines and the cries of strange children I separated self from other. I became hyper-vigilant, alert to every seeing, hearing and felt thing. I understood that all sorts of things went wrong, could go wrong, and adults who controlled everything that happened in the world could and did make mistakes.

## Plastered all the way from Paris

I am lying in my wooden cot in my bedroom in Moonee Ponds. The head of the cot is next to the window and I am watching the dust motes dance down, a breeze stirring the lace curtain through which the morning sun shines against shadow leaves on my ceiling. It is the morning of my third birthday.

I can tell you every little detail of my bedroom: the window has a wooden frame painted creamy white. Against the wall, at the end of my creamy-white wooden cot is my creamy-white wardrobe.

It has two slatted doors and my toy bag is hanging over one of the knobs. The bag is lumpy fat, pulled together by a drawstring. On the floor there's green lino with curvy patterns of dark green and red, two of my favourite colours. But I don't like the cold of the lino on my bare feet, not like the lounge-room carpet.

I know these memories are real and accurate because I've checked in with my mother. My family says I have an 'elephant memory', and it is unusual that I remember so much detail at such an early age. There is a neurological explanation as to why most people don't remember anything from early childhood. Freud believed early childhood memories were repressed and forgotten. Modern theorists believe infantile amnesia is a normal response to immature brain structures. The prefrontal cortex and the hippocampus are assumed to be crucial for the development of autobiographical memories and do not develop until the age of around three or four. The hippocampus can also be affected by trauma where a child disassociates or refuses to think about the trauma and therefore memories are not well recorded or easily retrieved.

I suspect something else was going on in my early life. Given the trauma experienced as a result of my condition you'd think I'd remember less rather than more than the average infant. However, I suspect my trauma was not so complex as to develop serious consequences for perception, function and behaviour. I was born into a family environment where I was loved and cared for, which I'm sure is a mitigating factor. I suspect it was being born with acute and chronic pain that led to me being hyper-observant, that the pain messages to my brain caused it to sharpen focus from a very early age.

Next to my wardrobe, to the right of my cot, is my creamy-white door. I see the knob turn. Mum and Dad creep in, crouched low. They are pushing something under a green sheet and singing *Happy Birthday*. Dad sweeps the sheet away and there is a shiny red metal tricycle with yellow wheels. Dad is sitting me on the cold metal seat and Mum is placing my bare feet on the pedals. 'Now push!' I try with my left leg. It's the strongest. But it's still hard for my foot to push the wheel forward. I grip hard, my lax toes curving round the pedal like a monkey. I get it moving. Dad steers me away from the wall out into the hallway and I'm off.

Before my third birthday I had been ensconced in plaster. On and off and on again and re-plastered, repaired on the kitchen table. At first it wasn't about broken bones, it was about trying to get my hip joints in place. I was sculpted in plaster from the waist down and my hip joints permanently flexed so that my feet ended up round my ears. A wooden beam was fixed in between my legs so the plaster didn't move and crack. Any more plastering and I could have been mistaken for a Pompeii victim suspended in solidified magma.

Lower to the ground I slid along on a stuffed toy dog on wheels. It had a flat, furry acrylic back and I would lie on my tummy, rest my chin on its head and push myself along the floor with my arms. I took the dog to hospital, speeding along the wide polished floors, bumping into the walls like a dodgem car. I whizzed past the wooden rocking horse with its tail made of real horsehair and hoped I could ride on it when the plaster came off. But it was never off for long enough.

The smell of wet plaster of Paris is still in my nostrils—that dank, musty-fresh smell oozing from the plastered bandages as Mum pulled them from the packet and rested them in a bowl of warm water. Slap, slap and sliding into place, patching up and patting out so they covered the curves without lumps or dents. I put my hands in the warm milky-with-plaster bowl and helped pat it all down. There'd be a watery mess from here to Kingdom Come. I wasn't let down until the carapace had hardened. If it was cold, I lay in my old bassinet in front of the gas fire in the dark lounge-room to dry rock hard. When no one was looking I prodded the soft bits with my fingers, leaving little marks.

Mum took me to the shops and on the train in a large baby's pram. I always looked my best though no fancy bonnet was going to detract from my feet yanked up and plastered close to my ears. I didn't know any better and for Mum it was just how it was. So, when a passing woman asked what was wrong with the baby in the pram why would my mother say anything but, 'She's fine. Just got a bit of a cold.' Which was the truth.

And why would she not wonder why the woman looked horrified? Normal is in the eye of the beholder.

Plaster was both friend and enemy. Limbs forced to remain still for even a week weaken muscles and no weight-bearing weakens bones, but bones must be stilled to heal. I became a frozen paradox. When the metal scissors broke through the plaster, I would shake like a jellyfish because it felt like everything was going to water swimming in an ocean of air. Then another break, another plaster on, another plaster off, another break. I was put in the sun on a thin mattress on the grass to get vitamin D on my lily-livered limbs. I rolled off and snap! Gravity, that heavy-handed beast, had won again. It's a wonder I didn't spontaneously collapse from the inside out. If the ocean wasn't so cold, I'd float there forever nibbling on seaweed. My legs would never break. I'd grow a fin and become a mermaid.

As soon as I could stand on my skinny, uneven legs long enough to walk without breaking, Mum took me to a photo-graphic studio. I sat on a bench of white fur wearing a red and black paisley dress she'd made. It had long sleeves and was finished off with a white yoke collar. Mum loved bold statements. No wishy-washy-wavering-pale-watercolours! My hair had been pulled into a topknot, a sprouted mushroom tied off with a red satin ribbon. At first, the cameraman had put a pale blue sky behind me but Mum shooshed it away. She chose a backdrop of olive green that echoed the hazel of my eyes and the olive in my skin. She wanted me to look bold and strong. I looked like a miniature adult—full of knowledge and expectation, understanding everything and nothing.

## Unblinking eyes in the headlights of destruction

The doll has blonde wavy hair in pigtails, wide blue eyes, a red and white gingham dress with a white apron round her waist. She's just the right size to hold in my hand. Her arms and legs move in their plastic sockets. I stare into her pretty unblinking eyes and tell her I hate her. I sit her hard on the bookcase in my bedroom, her legs splayed straight out like they are in plaster. But they aren't in plaster; she just doesn't have knees. I lie on my bed and try to outstare her, but those blue eyes stay unblinking.

The doll reminds me of that stupid Elly May, on *The Beverly Hillbillies* TV show. She has the same silly curly hair in pigtails and a dress like Elly May. Every time I look at her an angry monster stirs in my guts. I hate her so much I haven't even given her a name.

'Well, I think she's a very pretty doll, but if you don't want her, she'll go to a poor family where she'll be appreciated.'

It makes me hate her even more thinking some other little girl might like her, or even love her. Why should my doll go to a loving home? She'd like that, wouldn't she, sitting in another little girl's bedroom, getting all the lovey-dovey attention, and then her cutesy-wutesy curly hair and big blue eyes would win!

Guilt slides out of my guts and snakes round. I know that feeling because of the trick I played on Mum when I didn't want to clean my teeth. I hadn't really lost my toothbrush; I'd hidden it in the back of the bathroom drawer. I thought it was funny but Mum told me that to lie was a bad thing to do. Mum was worse than angry; she was very disappointed. I didn't know a trick could be a lie.

I'm not anything like my doll. Sometimes when I go to the hospital people tell me or Mum I'm 'cute', a 'pretty little girl'. But I'm not a doll or a puppy dog or a stuffed toy.

I hate it when people put on that voice. I stare back at them and try not to blink. I don't smile, I just look. I stare at them like I do with my doll until they look away. I'm used to looking. I look round the waiting room. We wait a long time on the long wooden bench full of people. It's hard work getting here. We must come all the way into the city on the train to see the specialist. He's the one who's meant to look after my bones. We spend ages and ages and ages waiting with all the other families. I hate it when the babies cry. I'm so bored but I don't talk to anyone. I don't like talking to people I don't know. Mum ends up chatting to some families who speak differently to us and have lots of children. This is what we have to do when it isn't an emergency. Sometimes I wish it would be an emergency, but I only think that for a little minute. I look at the adults who start talking to each other when they're not dealing with the children. Some of the women have scarves on their heads. Some men are here too, but Dad hasn't come with us because he is at work.

My doctor tells me to take my dress off and walk up and down and up and down. Sometimes he pulls at my skin and opens my eyes and shines a light in them. Mum asks him some questions, but I can see he really wants to open the other door in his room because he stands there with his hand on the other door's doorknob. There's another family on the other side waiting for him to come in. Then he asks Mum to put my clothes back on and we go home.

Mum says my doll might go to one of the poor families in the waiting room. There are little girls there who don't have any dolls, let alone one as pretty as mine.

I grab my doll and look into her face and the monster comes back. I hate her so much I get a texta and scribble all over her stupid face. Then I pull her head off. And tear off her dress. She's naked except for her tiny underpants. I want to pull off her arms and legs, but something stops me.

Mum's disappointed again. And a bit angry. The guilt is all mixed up with how good the monster felt when I did those things. I've done it now. I'm not allowed to keep the doll any more, even if I change my mind. I have to scrub the texta off her face before she goes in the box with some clothes and other things Mum's going to send to the poor family. I tuck Samuel, my teddy that I got when I was a baby, under the blankets with me. He's cuddly like a pillow. When I wake up, I pretend my hot water bottle, which isn't hot anymore, is a big man with a little head and I speak to it in a secret language. I put a singlet on it, and a jumper. He is very smart and I'm glad his head's too small for a face.


## The dangers of eating with grandparents

1965. Our newly built home in Aspendale smelled of polished wooden boards and freshly painted plaster. The streets were pale concrete and every house had neat front lawns hiding the soggy clay beneath. After rain, the grass would squish when you walked on it and when it rained too much a big truck with a thick black hose would come and suck out our septic tank. Closer to the house my parents had laid pale loose stones, which was the fashion and perhaps kept the damp from invading the walls. The only plant growing among the stones was a large cactus. The only trees stood at the end of our street behind the high cyclone fence of the local golf course. Behind us were paddocks with cows that scratched themselves along our back fence and dropped steaming pats.

Once we'd settled in, Grandma from Queensland decided to visit. She was my Dad's Mum who I'd never met before. Mum had been in a tizz all day, cooking and cleaning and making sure everything was 'just so'. We had to make a good impression, she said.

Dad pulled into the driveway in our newly acquired second-hand green and white Holden sedan. I pulled open the front door. Grandma was all skin and bone. She squinted hard at me with pinprick eyes and moved her mouth into something between a smile and a grimace. Then she sniffed the air and screeched, 'What's that AWFUL SMELL?!'

I couldn't smell an awful smell but Grandma smelled like an old wardrobe.

Dad plonked her on the modular lounge and followed Mum into the kitchen. It was very quiet in there. I sat and smiled at Grandma. I couldn't think of anything to say.

'I'm old', she said. 'I've got thin blood. It makes me cold. HAROLD! Get me a blanket for my knees, I'm freezing.'

I was confused because the air felt warm to me. Dad came into the lounge room and fussed until she was settled with a rug tucked round her that my other Nana had crocheted. I wondered if Grandma was so grumpy because she had my bones, all achy and breaky. Mum came in a few minutes later. Her eyes were red. She announced dinner was served. Grandma wasn't impressed; she'd just gotten comfortable. Dinnertime was very quiet. Dad tried to make a bit of conversation, but it fizzled and landed in the middle of the table like a damp firecracker. When Mum announced dessert was rice pudding, Dad's favourite, Grandma just grunted.

'Not as good as mine,' she said.

After Grandma, Mum's Dad, the tailor, came to visit. He had a rubbery face, sticky-out ears, and hair swept thinly across the top of his head. He offered to take me for a stroll in my pusher before dinner. I was too old for a pusher, but I couldn't walk as far or as fast as other kids my age. It had been raining and the place was sodden, but Mum didn't protest. She had plenty to do before Dad came home from work.

Beyond the driveway there were few footpaths. There were houses across the road but there were also many gaps where blocks had been cleared for other new houses to be built. Our stroll started out bumpy and didn't get much better. Grandpa carved deep crevices with my pusher and a few times we became stuck.

'Where do you want to go?' he asked.

'I dunno.'

'How 'bout we go to the milk bar and I'll buy you an ice-cream.'

I knew Mum wouldn't be happy about this because it was almost dinnertime but who was I to say no to Grandpa? It took ages to get to the milk bar. Grandpa parked me outside while he went in. The wheels of the pusher left clumps of mud all over the footpath.

We wended our way home as I held the drumstick tight and licked around the top and the sides until I reached the half soggy crunchy cone. It was getting dark and it seemed to take a lot longer to get back than it did to get to the shops. I think Grandpa might have got a bit lost but he called it an adventure so I wasn't nervous. And it gave me time to finish the ice-cream before we got home so it could be our secret.

The cold air pinked up my face, but what started out as a warm, flushed feeling in my cheeks began turning into something hot and itchy, a rash creeping its way down my forehead and neck then slowly across my arms. By the time Grandpa and I returned Mum was frantic and I was covered in red welts.

'Where have you been! ... Oh my God, what did you feed her!!!??'

'It was just a bloody drumstick, fa Chrissake!'

I suddenly felt guilty. I didn't want Mum to know because she'd tell me off for ruining my appetite.

'Well, a drumstick has peanut sprinkles and I told you she's allergic to peanuts!!'

'Well, it's not going ta bloody kill her!' were Grandpa's last words on the peanut-induced rash.

Mum left him with some cotton balls and a bottle of calamine lotion while she went to serve the dinner I no longer had an appetite for.

I'd spent so much time in disinfected hospitals my immune system didn't seem to have much muscle. I was allergic to peanuts, eggs, cats, dogs, horses, grass pollens, dust. I'd start out with a sneeze that would become a cold that would become bronchitis and sometimes pneumonia. Oftentimes, after I was discharged from hospital, Mum's instincts would kick in and she'd try and grubby me up, pushing me to make mud pies in the backyard with her. I needed more exposure to germs, she said. I hated it. All I wanted to do was go inside and wash my hands. Hospital had trained me into spotlessness, swathed in fresh, starched white sheets every morning, lying in a metal cot so shiny I could see my reflection.

The next time I saw Grandpa I was in hospital again. He arrived with an icy pole in the shape of a rocket. The icy pole was so cold Grandpa struggled to get the paper off but it was so much yummier than the hospital's rubbery jelly and melty ice-cream and it was just the right size to wrap my whole mouth around so nothing dripped on the sheets. When I'd finished, Grandpa said I had raspberry lipstick lips. He took the stick and told me he'd be back in a couple of days with another icy pole. But it was the last time I saw him because he went to Heaven instead.

## Scarred for life

Mum was polishing our wooden floors with the electric twin-brush polisher. We were still saving to afford carpet. The polisher made a loud, whooshing sound that vibrated happily in my ears. The sound could have been the smiling cleaners in their white overshoes polishing the shiny lino in the hospital. I danced and hummed down the hallway, turning to face the  front door, the lounge to the left, my room with the pale pink walls to the right.

Mum followed down the hallway, thrumming and swishing. Then bam! I was on my bum in a blink and the screams in my head had me knowing something was broken. Very, very broken. I screamed high as the motor shuddered and stopped. I wanted Mum to help but I screamed DON'T TOUCH ME! with the fear of knowing something had to happen and knowing it would mean even more pain.

Mum's friend wavered in front of me as I sucked on a plastic tube. Everything went fuzzy. I heard them talking in a far-away tunnel. The orange piece of cellophane I had slipped on glinted on the lounge floor. I remembered slipping before in that same cellophane spot and being asked if my leg was broken. I remembered nodding and Mum believing me because I always felt the difference between a bruise and a break. A bruise is a heavy, thumpy thud and a break cuts sharp and twitches if you move. If I'd had the words, I could have written an encyclopaedia of pain—the pain of a finger in a door, of an insect bite, an ear pulled, an ankle twisted, a collarbone snapped, hot water, fire.

The ambulance took off down the Nepean Highway to the other side of town. I lay flat, keeping my breath shallow and wincing with every shift of the ambulance's low-slung suspension. I didn't dare move, even to wipe the tears pooling in my ears. Next to me sat an old man who told me about fairies dancing up his chimney when he lit a fire. I imagined fairies dancing up his hairy nose. Dashes of water hit the windows. Trees and clouds swept past. Streetlights multiplied. Stop and start, stop and start. I closed my eyes. The metallic smell of buses and trucks and the grinding noise of machines told me we were moving through the city.

I lay propped on cold, plastic-covered pillows in a metal cot with the sides up. The fall had dislocated my left hip and broken my left leg in three places. The doctor, very tall in his white coat, leaned on the bars and told me I must have an operation to fix my leg, but I wouldn't feel anything because they would give me something to make me sleep. But I was sure I still felt things in my sleep. An operation meant they would go inside my leg. It would be just like a magic trick. Ta da! We'll fix your leg while you are sleeping and you won't feel a thing!

I waited for Dad. A nurse brought some blue medicine in a little cup. She watched me as I swallowed it then told me I shouldn't eat or drink anything more until after the operation. Then Dad was there leaning over the bars and giving me a kiss on my forehead and pulling up a chair. Another nurse came into the ward. She moved from cot to cot with golden medicine and a little square of chocolate to slide it down with. When she came to me, I said, 'But I've had the blue medicine.'

I looked to Dad to reinforce the blue-medicine-rule. But he smiled at the singsong smiling nurse then looked at me and said, 'Now you have to do what the nurse tells you. She knows what you should do.'

I drained the measuring cup and put my tongue out for the chocolate square.

The orderlies unlocked the wheels on my cot and took me round and down corridors. Whish, whish, the vomit rose from my throat onto my cheeks, through my hair onto the sheets.

'I told her I had the blue medicine,' I said to the ceiling.

The doctor was right, I didn't remember feeling anything until I opened my eyes and ta da! There I was, my left leg in plaster, right up my thigh. The pain was deep inside and the outside was hard and itchy and I wanted to scratch and scratch but it was impossible to get to the itch deep down in that plaster of Paris. A nurse arrived with a long plastic scratching spoon. I wanted to yank that spoon out of her hand and scratch exactly where it itched.

'Watch out for the metal sticking out,' I told her.

But who listens to a four-year-old in a cot? She smiled and after scratching away she picked me up and I screamed in her ear. There was a metal wire coming out from the side of my leg that was wedged into the plaster. Now there was a bloodied tear in my thigh and a nurse with no smile. A metal plate had been put in my leg. The metal wire had been put there to help keep my hip in the right place. The doctors had given Mum some powder in a puffer that she put down the plaster. If I started to smell like rotting meat, she must tell them. I didn't want to be meat. I didn't want to rot and smell like the dead possum in our roof. I wanted to be clean, clean and far away.

My bones were like the soft lead encased in wooden pencils. Cracks sprung where the plate ended and then I fractured under the plate. The X-ray couldn't see through the plate and the doctors didn't believe Mum when she told them my leg was broken.

It had taken me a while to feel the break. I remember lying in bed and Mum bringing me an eggnog, the egg and milk and honey and cinnamon she gave me when I didn't feel like eating. Being in bed during the day gave me mixed feelings. I liked resting and feeling safe, being looked after, but I hated being sickly and being left out. I could hear other kids playing outside. I remember Mum starting up the vacuum cleaner and feeling lonely and comforted at the same time. The humming vibrated like a song. I fevered and sweated with it all and swished my head back and forth. The pain spilled beyond the head-swishing, the humming became groaning. I stared into Mum's worried face.

'It's broken,' I said, 'it's hurting too much.'

After the plate was taken out and I recovered, the stitches were cut and then pulled like when Mum unstitched a hem. I could feel the thick string being tugged out from beneath my skin. Some of the bits stuck. They wanted to stay in my leg. They'd been in my body so long they thought they were part of me. I wanted to look, but I didn't because then I wouldn't have to look at it in my mind over and over.

I wish the doctors could do a magic trick and ta da! Away the scar. I don't like looking at it and remembering. A scar never forgets itself.

## A grumpy old man and two guns

Five days before I turned four, my brother, Kenton, was born. He was a chubby baby with a naughty, toothless grin.

Kenton could move in ways I never could. As soon as he could manage, he was scaling the back fence, getting splinters stuck in his bare feet. He ran and ran and peeled the shells off garden snails and chewed on their slimy bodies, grinning at the disgust on my face. At two years of age he went through a kicking phase. He kicked me, Mum, the walls. She tied my brother's legs together and sat him on top of the wardrobe in their bedroom. If he kicked then he would have done a Humpty Dumpty. I was worried but he was cool, sitting up there grinning down at me when I went in to check before Mum finally took him down.

Inside our new house Mum chose modern, fashionable interiors created to last a lifetime. An alta moda of furnishings. There was the modular corner lounge suite built with a hardwood frame and covered in Italian silk fabric, a check pattern shot with pink, blue and aqua. She bought a large lamp to go on the Scandinavian occasional table she placed next to the modular lounge. The base had been imported from Italy. It was cream ceramic with fine grey lines in a crackling pattern. The lampshade was made of aqua silk to go with the aqua in the lounge fabric and the aqua curtains. I wasn't allowed to touch the lamp so, when no one was looking, I did. The pattern made it look textured but it was actually very smooth. But that wasn't what caused the calamity.

It was my brother's fault. Sort of. I chased him along the polished floorboards on my knees (we were still saving up for the wall-to-wall carpet) and, squealing with excitement, he bumped into Scandinavia and Italy came crashing down. Mum raced from the kitchen, still clutching a tea towel, and screamed, 'I told you not to touch that lamp! It's VERY EXPENSIVE!! Oh, my God!!'

'We didn't touch it, Mummy,' I said with conviction, because we hadn't. 'It just fell all by itself!'

Mum had tears in her eyes as she picked the shards off the floor.

'I'll have to glue it back together, BUT IT WILL NEVER BE THE SAME!!'

I wanted Mum to be angrier. It was hard to know where to put her despair. Once it had been all put together again, just like Humpty Dumpty, it did look the same, pretty much, because the glued bits blended into the grey pattern that looked like cracked glaze. Except for one little chip, which Mum turned to the wall. Everyone who visited admired the lamp but, like all family secrets, the imperfection was hidden and never mentioned. I wondered if my bones also looked like cracked ceramic and left little chips when I broke.

Kenton and I played outside a lot after that. Mum made him a fishing rod from a piece of dowel and some fishing line with a magnet tied to the end. She added fish shaped from tin cans in a large bucket of water and he caught the fish with his magic magnetic rod. I played cubbies in the A-framed cubby house made from corrugated iron until Mum found redback spiders nesting in the wooden beams. I couldn't go back in until the fumes from the Mortein spray had cleared and Mum had collected all the little black and red bodies and put them in the bin.

We were still waiting for carpet when a weeny little house called a granny flat was built in our backyard. It was a big backyard and we didn't have much in it except for the Hill's Hoist, my cubby house and a sandpit in the corner the stray cats kept pooing in. One cat was feral. It hid under the granny flat foundations and when I poked my hand under there, it bit me on the wrist. I had blood pouring from the tooth holes. Mum took me to the doctor for a tetanus shot and we found out the cat had broken my wrist. I came home with my arm bandaged to a board. Not long after, I broke my collarbone when I tried to climb up the outside of my cubby house. Then my arm was put in a sling. The pain was awful: every time I breathed or moved it caught me like I imagined a knife would if I'd been stabbed. The sling round my neck rubbed up against my collarbone but without the sling the weight of my arm pulled on the fracture. I couldn't sleep for weeks. The pain encompassed everything to the point where I didn't even think to protest.

Once the granny flat was completed an old man called Gooley from my Mum's hometown came to stay. Mum was being a 'Good Samaritan,' she told me quietly. Gooley was down on his luck, a war veteran, and it made him very grumpy. I reckoned I was a war veteran too and it made me grumpy as well. But we didn't have much in common. Every morning Gooley shuffled into our kitchen to eat an enormous bowl of porridge that looked like his face, all pudgy and lumpy and grey. He didn't have many teeth and sometimes he slobbered down his front all over the napkin Mum tucked into his collar before he started slurping.

When old Gooley took afternoon naps in the granny flat, Kenton and I tried to sneak a look through a crack in the blinds.

If we made even a skerrick of a noise, we'd be told to PISS OFF YA MONGRELS. This made us giggle and we'd start tapping on the windows. Mum finally caught us out when she burst through the back door with a basket full of washing.

'Inside, you two. Now!'

She went in to see the old man. I snuck out and eavesdropped on their conversation. Mum did most of the talking. She said we were just children and he shouldn't swear at us. No one was allowed to swear in our house, she said, especially not in front of the kids. After that Gooley would sulk for hours with his tinny radio tuned loudly to the races.

When the ambulance arrived in the driveway, I thought it must have been for me because it was always for me but this time it was for Gooley. I watched from the back step. The ambulance men wheeled the trolley bed round to the granny flat and old Gooley came out with a large hankie over his mouth. I could see it hurt for him to cough, just like when I had pneumonia. A sick feeling started in my guts, that feeling of needing to cough but trying not to because it hurt so much.

I had pneumonia a lot and became feverish and struggled to breathe. The thick white penicillin needled into my bum hurt like hell. Once, I felt so ill I almost gave up. I was six years old with double pneumonia and collapsed lungs. I could have just flown away, breathing free, never breathing again, no more pain, away, away. But I chose to come back to be in my future.

Gooley looked greyer than his porridge. I saw his eyes turn my way then slide off into the distance.

'Where are they taking him, Mummy?' I asked.

'He's going to a hospital called Heidelberg Repat.'

I didn't know that hospital; I was always taken to a hospital in the city.

Heidelberg Repat. had covered walkways between buildings and multi-coloured lines on the footpath that led you to different places, and rows of pipes that snaked along the walkway ceilings, just like the underground part of my hospital. But in this hospital the smells were different with overcooked cabbage and stale pee instead of disinfectant and plaster. Old Gooley was in a room with three other men. One had yellow skin and eyes and one was so skinny I could see all the bones in his face. Old Gooley had an oxygen mask over his mouth and the steam made a hissing sound. I hated wearing those masks. The nurses always told me it was to help me breathe but it felt like the opposite and I always wanted to pull it off. But Gooley looked like he didn't care one way or the other. His eyes slid around the room though I could tell he wasn't really looking.

Old Gooley never came back to the granny flat. Looking inside it made me feel sad. I could feel the old man's loneliness in the walls, in the few miserable belongings he'd left behind. Mum put everything into a big plastic garbage bag and vacuumed the place before she locked the door.

Not long after, it was Kenton's third birthday and he got a black machine gun. It made one hell of a racket and coloured sparks flew out when you pressed the trigger. Just as well Gooley had died by then or it might have done him in. We were all shot dead several hundred times in the first hour. I wanted a gun, too. I was so excited when my seventh birthday came five days later, and a gun-shaped present was handed to me. I ripped off the paper in gleeful anticipation. It was a gun made of lacquered wood painted in bright enamel stripes. Pretty and completely ineffectual. Its ammunition, the ultimate humiliation, was a cork attached to a string that you shoved into the barrel like a cork in a wine bottle. A trigger pushed the cork out with a puff of air and a little plop that had it swinging like a dead man hanging. Nowhere to go but down. It barely even made a sound.

I wasn't just jealous then because Kenton could run and do things my body couldn't do, I was jealous because he was a boy with a real pretend gun and I was a girl with an unreal pretend gun that couldn't even make a proper gun noise.

# SALAD DAYS
## (Without the dressing)

**Hold on to the Jesus strap!**

The Principal stood on the wooden platform in her long white habit with a large cross around her neck. We sat up straight behind our desks, arms outstretched, hands clasped just as the teacher taught us in our prep grade. From the folds of her gown, the Principal produced two items: her right hand held a monkey puppet with a jelly baby in its hands, and in her left hand an enormous leather belt with a large brass buckle. Her smile was brief and conditional.

'Now, children, in my right hand you can see a very good monkey. The right hand is the hand of God. And if you are good, you will be rewarded.'

We stared as the Principal wiggled the monkey's arms and the jelly baby danced. A couple of children giggled.

'Now, in my left hand is the STRAP!'

She lifted the belt and cracked it on the platform. We flinched.

'The left hand is the hand of the Devil and the Devil is evil. And if you are bad, you will be punished. It is up to you to decide whether you follow the path of the right hand or the path of the left. Hands up who is going to be like the good little monkey.'

Our hands shot up. The Principal pulled a packet of jelly babies from her robes and had the monkey hand them to the teacher to distribute.

I worried about holding crayons and pencils in my left hand. When I tried to use my right hand, it felt all wobbly and wrong. Did being left-handed mean I was evil? Did the things I drew come from the Devil's hand? I kept myself as small as possible to avoid all the questionable bad things that could get me into trouble.

Now, if you did something bad but you didn't know that you were doing something bad at the time did that count? I was drinking from one of the school fountains when a boy in my class came up and dared me to climb the pipes that formed an X on the wall next to me. Above the pipes there were two little windows and he said I would see something very special if I climbed up and took a peep through them.

'I dare you,' he said.

With the help of the boy, I secured my foot in the crook of the X and pulled myself up.

'Can you see?' he asked.

I stretched and grabbed each pipe until I managed to get a look through the crack in one of the windows. Below was a room with a row of doors. I heard a flush and a teacher appeared. She moved to the sink on the opposite wall and washed her hands. I gasped and almost fell backwards. The boy clutched his stomach and laughed.

'Did ya see her poo?'

I slithered down as quickly as I could until I felt the relief of solid ground. A flush of guilt hit as I realised I'd been tricked into peeking into the teacher's toilets. Just before the bell rang the boy dobbed me in to the teacher on yard duty. She didn't believe I didn't know what I'd been doing. I walked into class with the bell ringing in my ears like the bell of doom and the image of that giant strap belting the back of my legs. *Surely the teacher wouldn't*. I was called up onto the platform. The teacher produced a feather duster with a bamboo handle. She told me to put both my hands out, palms up. I looked across to all my classmates safely behind their desks. The boy who'd tricked me threw me a sly grin. I could feel tears coming but was determined not to give him the satisfaction of crying. The feather duster came down and instinctively I pulled my hands away. Some of my classmates twittered. I closed my eyes. I could tell by the force of the sting the teacher wasn't hitting me as hard as she could. Still, the three strikes hurt enough and left red marks. I knew then that in between the right hand of good and the left hand of evil there was a big ball of grey.

Our first-grade teacher was nice until she wasn't. She must have been pushed by the Devil's hand. It was summer and all the boys were bare-legged. She told a boy to come up to the platform then called on the rest of us to come up and form a circle around him. Apparently, he'd been kicking kids in the playground and wouldn't stop. She ordered us to kick him in the shins all at once. He started yelping like an injured dog. The more he cried the more the teacher pushed us to 'give him a good kick so he knows what it feels like.' I stood back. I tried to make myself invisible. But the teacher saw me and made others stand back so I could get closer.

'Go on, kick him,' she ordered.

I looked down at my feet, stood on my goodish leg and tipped the front of my shoe forward. I barely made contact but I'd done as I was told. It was only then the teacher ordered us back to our desks, leaving the shin-bruised bully whimpering out front. I couldn't imagine Jesus dishing out such a cruel punishment but I could imagine the Principal might. Did this mean the Principal was the Devil in disguise?

In grade two a very, very bad thing happened to one of my classmates. She was a tiny thing, small like me, but wizened like a dried-up doll. She had black hair set in something between a bob and a bowl cut and her skin was like pulled parchment with little lines under her blue-grey eyes. It happened on a weekend while she was playing hide-and-seek. Looking for the perfect place to hide, she went out onto the street and slid into the gutter under a parked truck. There, she huddled, waiting for her older sister to come looking. The noise of the truck's engine must have shocked her into moving but not quick enough to avoid a tyre rolling over her. She was rushed to hospital and by Monday word was out: the girl who sat opposite me in class wasn't going to be coming back anytime soon. She had tubes all over, it was touch and go. Her older sister, at least one class ahead, a ruddy-faced girl with hair as red as her sister's was black, walked round the school yard at break times in a daze, as if she were her sister's ghost. We gawped from a distance. She was as 'other' as her sister on life support. Weeks, then months went without the empty seat in my class being filled. And after a while no one spoke about her. Her empty classroom chair had me thinking of the times I had to miss school to be in hospital. Just as our class had written get-well letters to her so I had received get-well letters. Only special kids got get-well letters. She was my shadow twin in abnormality. If God and his son Jesus and the Holy Ghost loved us so much, why did they let things like this happen? I wondered about that a lot. Perhaps sometimes good and bad things got wound together like a plait so it was difficult to tell which hair belonged where.

### Racing through little school doing things I couldn't do and shouldn't try

It was difficult not to stand out as I was pushed through the school gates in an oversized baby's pram. It was the old-fashioned type with giant wheels, a woven basket exterior and a fancy cloth hood. I liked to think of it as my chariot. It was a safe way to get around after the plate in my left leg had been removed after the surgeon realised it was failing to prevent more fractures. The fact that a fracture was confirmed under the plate itself proved the point.

'Be gentle with her,' the grade one teacher said to my class-mates, 'She's fragile.'

That's what cardboard boxes say when there's something breakable inside.

Girls in my class took dibs to push me around. At break times, when the teachers weren't looking, there were exhilarating running-against-the-pram races. I was pushed so fast the air rushed in my ears. Sometimes I won. It felt like the next best thing to running and, even though I didn't much like being the centre of attention, it felt good to be fitting in. But when my chariot made a sharp U-turn on the netball court and I fell out the game was up. It hurt a bit but I didn't cry and was rewarded with streams of daisy chains picked off the footy oval by the girls. I rolled into class looking like a piñata on wheels.

Once my leg was fully healed, I whizzed to school on my tricycle, alternating between seated pedalling and standing on the bar between the pedals and pumping the left pedal with my one goodish leg. I would have preferred a 'normal' two-wheeler but, even with trainer wheels the risk of falling was too great. I put my schoolbag in the basket on the front, held the handlebars tight and mostly rode on the footpath. In winter I rode with my red, white and black beanie-scarf. Other kids on their way to school walked around me or ran past. I usually ignored them but one morning a boy turned and, walking backwards ahead of me he yelled, 'So, what team do ya barrack for?'

'Aw, she must barrack for St Kilda with that scarf!' cried another boy rushing past.

'Um, yeah, St Kilda,' I said.

I may not have played sports but I ran in my dreams. I ran to escape scary monsters, I ran on the beach, I ran up stone castle stairways, I ran to feel the air pull the curls from my face. And I also flew above the school playground over the basketball rings, over roofs, close to the clouds.

The callipers I was fitted with at eight years old gave me extra confidence even though I hated wearing them. They looked so ugly attached to leather ankle boots, the sort I used to wear as a younger kid. The inside of the boots had a wedge of leather with a buckle fixed around a metal rod. The rod was wedged inside the boot heel and rose along the outside of my calf to my knee where it was fitted with a padded cuff and another buckle. I could step forward with my feet and ankles properly aligned for the first time. It was hoped the contraption would retrain the muscles in my feet.

I don't remember any other child at the school having a physical disability. It was the 1960s before the concept of integration, political correctness and inclusivity. Then, it didn't matter whether your disability was physical or mental; you were as special as the special school that would have you. But I was ensconced in the Catholic school system, I looked relatively 'normal' and I was smart. Tick, tick, tick.

The things I could do with my body made me a popular schoolyard attraction. I walked with a swivelling limp and could bend my wrists back so far that my thumb could touch my forearm. My elbows and knees bent backwards and I could twist my legs into poses only a trained ballerina could expect to achieve. Schoolmates loved it when I did my circus tricks. But when boys, who saw me as an easy target, were watching, the atmosphere changed. They would imitate my gait and call out grunting animal noises when no one else was around. Even so, now I had straight ankles and calves of steel I wanted to be in the class race. I wanted to compete just like I'd done in my chariot races.

White lines had been painted on the grassed oval for the running lanes. We all stood on the starting line, poised for the gun to shoot us forward. Mums and teachers were away to the left on seated platforms. Bang! And we were off. My classmates sped off and suddenly the lane looked to me like a never-ending green road. I couldn't even see the finish line. Instead, I looked down so I wouldn't trip. And I breathed so hard I felt dizzy. I pumped my arms hoping this would help propel me forward but I may as well have been a bird with clipped wings and a gnarly foot. I heard cheers and cries as first, second, third, fourth crossed the finish line. Eventually there was silence. I wanted to stop but I wasn't used to starting something I didn't finish, and I'd created my own momentum that was impossible to halt without stumbling. The race had finished but I hadn't finished the race. All I could hear was my breath and thumping blood. Everything fell away except me laying one callipered leg attached to one unyielding leather boot in front of the other.

I don't know how many minutes passed before I reached the finish line but I did, falling into the teacher who held me to a stop. There was a blasting cheer. My legs felt all wobbly and my skin was hot and cold and pink. I felt foolish. I wasn't normal on the outside and I wasn't normal on the inside. I was a stupid wind-up toy that made a clumsy start and couldn't stop itself tumbling over the edge unless someone picked it up. It was only in my imagination that I forgot the things I couldn't do and shouldn't try. How on earth did I think I could simply imagine running into existence?

## Sipping pink drinks in the war zone

1969. I'm eight years old and the doctors have something in store for me. For the first time I am sent to the Royal Children's Hospital instead of the children's ward of St Vincent's where I have always been treated. I'm told I am to be here for three weeks, which is a long time given I don't even have a fracture or a chest infection. I'm told I have to eat the same meal every day while I'm here. I'm given two choices: Vegemite sandwiches or chicken sandwiches. I choose chicken. Not a vegetable in sight.

I understand I will be given a large jug of pink fluid to drink first thing every morning. It is an experiment to see if my body can absorb extra calcium so my bones won't break so easily.

Mornings start very early in a hospital, the sun barely bouncing off the raised bars of my metal bed as the nurses waltz in with their giant laundry bags on wheels, their starched hats in place with bobby pins and their rubber-soled shoes squeaking on the forever-being-polished lino. The nurses dance their way into dawn with the radio playing songs about Vietnam. I have no idea of their significance but the songs stay with me: *Leaving on a Jet Plane*, *All Along the Watchtower*, *We Gotta Get out of This Place*, *Revolution*, and especially *Smiley*.

Being shaken awake before you've stopped dreaming feels so cruel. These smiling, enticing nurses never take no for an answer. Every morning, up, sitting out of bed, a HUGE jug of pink liquid calcium must go down my throat while my bed is remade into the neatest of starchy whiteness so stiff and cold and bright it takes hours to feel warm again. The liquid threatens to come up and destroy all the cleanliness. Full-up-to-pussy's-bow-with-no-room-left-for-Mrs-Manners. The only other thing I have to put in my mouth is a chicken sandwich. It's only the beginning of week two and even the smell of a chicken sandwich makes me nauseous.

My room has six beds. Opposite me is a girl who scares the bejesus out of me. She's sixteen with big breasts and hair between her legs. She's tall and imposing and, worst of all, she can't speak. A nurse tells me she is 'mentally retarded' but harmless. Tell that to an eight-year-old who wakes up with a big, tall girl in a loose nightie at the end of her bed, staring and grunting like an animal that wants something.

Diagonally opposite is a toddler with an enormous forehead and short limbs who is, I'm told, a dwarf. Then there is a pretty little Italian girl at the far end who's here for an operation, which has to be constantly postponed because her grandmother comes in and feeds her chocolates despite the nurses' stern words. I'd see grandma sneak them in her handbag and hand them to the girl when she thought no one was watching. But I always saw what she was up to. 'You'll make her sick!' I call out but Grandma always pretends she doesn't understand English.

Then there's the boy closest to me. I don't know what he's in for but he's pretty sick. The nurses are always fussing, pulling the green curtains round his bed and making him cry. Once I got up and saw his bare bum through a crack in the curtain. It was covered in red sores. I know he doesn't like crying in front of me but, of course, he has no choice. The green curtain does nothing to soak up any of our noises. I feel sad for him, especially as there's nothing wrong with me except being terribly bored with pink drinks and chicken sandwiches. His name is Graeme and he is about the same age as me. We never talk about the hospital stuff. We create our own world with his Superman, Spiderman and Batman dolls—and something like Lego he's brought in that interlocks to make plastic things like chains and bridges. We chain our beds together and act out stories from his comics. I have comics too, but they're the girly Disney ones full of Donald Duck and silly Minnie Mouse escapades. Graeme's comics are all about men with special powers who fight the baddies and save the world.

Graeme's bedridden most of the time, so it's up to me to keep things exciting. We discuss my missions against possible enemies. He shows me a little metal cannon that can shoot projectiles. We plan revenge on the Matron with the albatross headgear. She looks ridiculous stomping up and down the corridor with that white winged thing on her head. I decide to sacrifice a plastic hair comb for the task. The two of us twist off all its teeth for our arsenal. I let Graeme test the cannon first. He shoves in a plastic tooth and 'ping', it shoots across his bed to mine. A fair distance. Then it's my turn to ammo up and I take my place behind the door of our ward. I lie in wait, a tooth in the cannon, at the ready.

I hear the squeak of rubber on lino and sneak my head around the corner long enough to see who's coming. It's not the Matron, just one of the other nurses. Well, she can be the guinea pig. I line up my cannon and just as she passes, 'ping' I get her in the ankle.

'Oh, what's that?' she cries, giving a little skip.

Success! I'm sure she didn't see it coming. Then suddenly, arch enemy number one comes sailing past in full flight. This time I'm a bit more nervous but, determined to fulfil my mission, I strike. I see it hits her lower calf, but she sails on through as if nothing has touched her, not even the slightest twinge. Still, it felt very daring and I'd done it! I report back to base.

Matron stands in the doorway. We brace for an announcement.

'Now, children,' she says sternly, 'there is a brand-new show coming on the television in half an hour. It's usually past your bedtime but I've decided just for tonight I will keep the television on so you can watch *The Brady Bunch*.'

What sort of show would have Matron allow us to stay up specially to see it? We sit propped in our beds and crook our necks towards the black-and-white TV above the door frame as we are introduced to what we think is the most exciting kid's show ever. They have a big house and a maid and get up to all sorts of mischief that their Mum and Dad have to work out by the end of the half hour show. It is like an adult's show but for us kids. It is even better than *Skippy the Bush Kangaroo* and nothing like that show *M\*A\*S\*H* the adults watch but looks stupid to us. We tell our favourite nurses how much we love *The Brady Bunch* and they persuade Matron to let us watch it every night even though it is after our ridiculously early bedtime.

I've been on the pink drinks for more than a few days now and it's time to check my blood. The doctors try to squeeze a tube of it from my rolling-all-over-the-place veins. I don't have any control over what my veins do but they recoil like every other cell in my body. Surely, our bodies weren't designed to have needles stuck into us! Day after day the doctors get more desperate trying to extract my blood. In the end there is no place left unbruised except for my groin. This time the doctors take me out of the ward. They put me in a room and shut the door. They put me on a trolley. They pull my underpants down and spread my legs. My ankles are buckled into leather cuffs. I watch them grit their teeth and steady the needle. I scream. The pain is like fire. They hold me down hard. I can't even bend my knees. Wait 'til I tell Graeme. This is much worse than he ever gets. I'm sobbing great sooky sobs as they wheel me back. Everyone stares at me. I take one look at Graeme and realise I don't need to tell him a thing. Everyone's heard my screams, even though they shut the door and tried to cover my mouth. I don't blame the doctors. I could see they didn't like upsetting me, holding me down like that. They had to get the blood from me or there was no point in my being there. I hated my stubborn veins probably as much as they did.

It's time for Graeme to leave. He pulls back the plastic chain from between our beds and starts organising his toys. What am I going to do without him? I don't want him to leave. I feel like crying, but I don't. Graeme is happy to be going home. He fiddles around with all his stuff on the bed, the comics, the superheroes, the plastic links. Then he picks up the little cannon and passes it to me.

'For you,' he says, 'to protect you behind enemy lines.'

An occupational therapist arrives. She tells me there is a hospital school I can attend on another floor. I'm kind of happy having time away from school, but I'm so bored now that Graeme has gone, I agree to check it out.

'You'll meet all sorts of other children who are here, and they do some fun stuff,' she says too brightly.

Well, my idea of fun and a grown-up's idea of fun are usually two different things but as long as they don't make me weave baskets—something I hate doing—I'll go.

The hospital school is past the palliative care ward. I walk down the corridor, looking into rooms that have just a single bed in each of them. There are big windows so the patients can see what is going on around them. Almost every kid has wispy hair or is completely bald. Their eyes are big and old-looking. Not like an old person, like a young kid that knows more than most of us should know. Their skin is yellowy and their limbs skinny, all elbows and knees. Some of them have tubes coming out of their noses or their arms. They smile and wave as I go past. They wave like they are waving goodbye. I wave back and try to smile but my face feels all stiff. Each of them looks so calm. You can tell they know they are dying. Would I be so calm if I knew I was dying? I don't think so. I think I'd be really upset and probably angry. Unless I wanted to die, like the time when I was in hospital with double-pneumonia and collapsed lungs. I made the choice to live but I don't think these kids have made a choice to die. For the two weeks I walk back and forth to the school I see most of them disappear, replaced by another sickly new face.

'What happened to Sarah?'

'She died yesterday.'

I stop asking.

Hospital school is just as boring as I had imagined. There are so many of us at different ages that we all just do the simplest things like jigsaw puzzles and colouring in. I can't see the point. Putting together a dumb picture that's been cut into stupid shapes you have to fit back together only to pull it apart and put it back in the box when you're finished. Whoever thought that was a good idea? *Someone really stupid, that's who.*

It's almost time for me to go home. I think about counting how many chicken sandwiches I have to go but decide it's best not to think about it. I take a stroll down the corridor just off my room and I see a couple of the older teenage girls putting on lipstick and eye make-up. They look ridiculously excited.

'What's happening?' I ask one of the nurses.

'Oh, there's a very special visitor coming to the wards later. A pop star!'

'Is it Johnny Farnham? (I've just put in my secret diary that I love Johnny Farnham.) 'No, it's RONNIE BURNS!!'

Oh, that *Smiley* singer. I liked the sound of the song, but I didn't really know anything about him.

'Oh,' I say flatly.

There was no way I was going to go all silly like the older girls. Then there he was, Ronnie Burns sauntering down the corridor with a couple of other men. He had chopped-up wavy hair parted in the middle, a brown and white shirt with a big collar, a brown tank-top, flared pants and platform boots. The made-up girls squealed as he came closer. One even screamed like I'd seen on TV when The Beatles had come to town and everyone went crazy. I'd only been a tiny kid when that happened but, as usual, I'd been in hospital and we all sat around a TV to see the action. The noise was really irritating. Ronnie Burns grinned as he popped his head into each ward. The girls almost fainted. Some of them looked like they'd stopped breathing. I just stood looking gobsmacked at the reaction one man could produce in a bunch of teenage girls. He took one look at me, smiled and said, 'Hi, how'ya going?'

'Fine,' I said, through pursed lips, staring him down.

The only pop star I had time for was Johnny Farnham. Ronnie put a hand on my skinny eight-year-old shoulders and moved off to where the adoration really was. I bet Graeme wouldn't have been impressed, either.

# MEMENTO MORI
## (Hope and consequence)

### The good witch of holy places

1973. I lifted my fingers out of the water, the droplets poised mid-air as I brought my hands to my forehead, chest, shoulder then other shoulder in the sign of the cross. Such water was made holy with a priest's blessing but I doubted it was any more holy than what came out of our kitchen tap.

Mum and I moved through the entrance into the dark cave of the church. We were out of our diocese and it was a Saturday.

It felt strange to be in this unfamiliar church and surrounded by people looking so unwell. Everyone was coming to be healed, to be blessed by the mysterious woman at the altar who we were told had godly healing powers. But I knew from experience that healing from anything could be difficult and painful and sometimes impossible. Could she really heal me or any of these other people? There was a man with a greeny yellow face and sunken eyes who was struggling to walk. I walked with a limp but he was bent all over and looked like he might collapse at any moment. A large woman was being pushed in a wheelchair. There was a child with drooling lips all twisted inside a pram. Somewhere a baby was wailing as if it had been stuck with a pin. Beyond the familiar aromas of wood and incense rose the smell of sickly flesh as if the organs of some of these people were rotting inside them. I know that dying smell. It comes out of your skin and breath no matter how much you've been washed and had baby powder shaken over you. I've never actually seen a dead body but I've met people in hospital who were not going to make it out alive. I hope no one dies before they get to see the healer.

Mum squeezed my hand and pulled me into a pew. The countless rows ahead were full and the altar was far away but I knew the healer would be up there standing in front of Jesus hanging on the cross. I hated thinking about, let alone seeing that bedraggled, beatific body nailed to the cross. I could feel every nail being hammered into him. I have nightmares about it but I haven't told anyone.

I looked up at the massive wooden beams that crisscrossed the ceiling, defying gravity, all pointing to heaven. It's so dark anything could be hiding up there. A gargoyle. An angel. The souls of the dead. What if the souls couldn't get past the ceiling? They'd be all bouncing up there like helium balloons … balloons with texta faces looking very annoyed!

In the church it was so cold it felt damp. I was wearing a cardigan over my summer dress but my legs were bare. I swung them back and forth to keep the blood flowing and stop the boredom.

The pew was so hard on my hips, back, shoulders, neck, head: everything hurt more if I had to stay in the one position for too long. Mum knelt, clasped her hands and prayed with her eyes closed. I looked up to the ceiling. I wondered if feelings could live outside your body. Especially big feelings, like excitement or fear. Perhaps they went 'whoosh' up into the air. There could be a whole ball of everyone's feelings up in this ceiling. Jesus must have had lots of big feelings when he was up on the cross. I wonder if Jesus, or his father, God, or the Holy Ghost can hear me wondering?

I imagine the healer looks a bit like the good witch in *The Wizard of Oz*, with long robes like a priest and a sparkling gold stole matching her long golden hair. And she has a golden wand she places on the sick person's shoulders, and she makes their skin tingle ...

Then a miracle happened. The row in front stood, shuffled into the aisle and moved into the pew ahead. A man gestured for our row to get up. We walked, crab-like, into the aisle and edged our way forward to the next pew. And continued the long wait. I stood up to escape the hardness of the wood against the back of my legs. I knelt on the velvet-covered kneelers. I stood back up and leaned across Mum to get a view down the aisle. The two lines heading towards the altar were barely moving. This healing business takes a lot longer than getting communion. My bladder was almost full to bursting but Mum wouldn't let me look for the toilet on my own. I slumped back onto the pew. I threw my head back to the ceiling and hummed to myself, swinging my legs.

Then another miracle happened: a bell sounded for lunch. We left my cardigan behind to hold our spot, just as others had left pieces of clothing along the pews, all lying flattened just like the Wicked Witch of the West when her body disappeared inside her cloak with the tap of the Good Witch's wand. We moved with the crowd into the sudden brightness. Trestle tables and plastic chairs had been set out around a large shady tree in the courtyard and church ladies bustled around with large trays of sandwiches, platters of fresh fruit and little cakes and slices. I came back from the toilet, flapping the tap water off my washed hands, wriggled my way to a table, and grabbed a floppy paper plate. It was hard going, trying to balance two sandwich squares, a little bunch of grapes, a piece of cake and two chocolate slices altogether. I had to keep one hand flat under the plate and use my other hand to shield the pile from being elbowed to the ground by the crush of people all trying to do the same thing. Something struck the back of my legs and I nearly went down. It was a wheelchair coming through. A boy with a shaking body. He looked about my age. His Mum, well it's probably his Mum, was trying to feed him with a baby's bottle. He couldn't keep his head still and some of the liquid is spilled down his front. His Mum held the bottle to his mouth and a towel to catch the spills. It gave me a creeping feeling in my guts. That could be me. An old woman caught me looking at the boy. Her skin was pale and wrinkly like an albino crocodile.

Back inside, the church was as cool and dark as ever. It took a moment for my eyes to adjust. Mum knelt and closed her eyes in prayer. I felt bad wanting to pray about getting the hell out of there. I looked up to the ceiling. Is God up there? How could he see into so many souls at the same time? And why can't he just heal all of us 'whoosh!' like that so we can go home?

I imagined what it would be like if I was truly healed. I worried that if I didn't believe enough then I might stop a miracle from actually happening. There could have been people being healed up there at the altar but they never came back down the aisle because there was an exit up there too. It was in one door and out the other, with no proof of what magic might have taken place. How would it be if I was healed for real? I'd feel my hips moving out of their wrong positions. My pelvis would shift into the right mould and my back would straighten and I would feel all the creaking and cracking without any pain because everything would be reshaping into how it should have been all along. I would stand tall and for the first time ever I wouldn't hurt anywhere! I sat up as tall as I could with that vision of myself, chin up, shoulders back. I imagined the Good-Witch-healing-woman tapping me with her wand and my body glowing with warmth. I got down on the kneeler beside Mum and squeezed my eyes shut, and I prayed hard. The Good Witch, Peter Pan's Wendy and the priest all said it's a matter of faith. If you believed, it would happen. Maybe I just haven't been believing enough!

I imagined my body as strong and sturdy as the church. I would be trussed straight and tall, my legs columns of marble, my spine thrust against the gravity that crushed weaker things into the earth. I would be balanced and blessed.

Another pew forward. And another. The light through the stained-glass windows started to fade. I stood, I stretched, I sat. I swung my legs faster and faster to keep warm. I caught myself wanting to rock my head back and forth and hum as I did at home when I couldn't get to sleep. Mum looked like she'd just about had enough as well but we'd waited so long that leaving felt impossible. It was even more difficult for those with young kids. Some had been wrapped in rugs and had fallen asleep but then one would stir and cry, setting off others in a chorus of escalating distress. The noise echoed all around as desperate parents attempted to jiggle them back to rest. A couple in front packed up and left. A few others followed and suddenly, like the parting of clouds, I could see the altar. A few priests stood in robes and a row of people, some standing, some kneeling, some in wheelchairs were lined in front. Each priest laid his hands on the shoulders of the sick and mumbled some sort of blessing. Where is the healing woman, the golden-robed one?

As it darkened outside, the lights in the church were turned on. I rubbed my eyes and yawned away the anticipation, the boredom, the throng of the ill and desperate. A man came to our pew and whispered something to Mum. Mum stared straight ahead as she told me the healer had gone home. She looked deflated and I felt anger shoot through me.

I slumped and sulked. What kind of healer gives up like that? If we can wait this long, why can't she with her special powers? I knew I shouldn't have believed! I bet she was a fake and no one has been healed. What a joke! Mum interrupted my internal tirade. She said the priests at the altar were offering blessings instead and we should let them bless us before we went home.

I took her hand and walked awkwardly to the front of the altar and got stiffly onto my knees. I could feel tears begin and kept my head bowed so the priest who was coming forward to lay his hands on my shoulders would not mistake my distress for gratitude. I felt a steady pressure on my shoulders as the priest mumbled the usual 'in-the- name-of-the-Father-Son-and-Holy-Ghost' routine. I felt no tingle, no transformation, no shift in my body. My anger raged and splintered. Anger at Mum for bringing me here in the first place, anger at myself for even contemplating a possible miracle, anger at wasting a sunny Saturday, anger for the whole church and all its people being hoodwinked. These priests and that holy woman are all liars and they should all go to jail! Then I looked towards Mum who was kneeling beside me and I saw she had tears in her eyes too. She helped me up, took my hand and gave it a little squeeze as we walked away into the darkness. There were no words, just the sadness of a mother who'd hoped for the best and a frustrated eleven-year-old girl who didn't know how to offer comfort.

## Humans are animals are humans

Lyn-don't-call-me-Lynette Little stood at the counter waiting for the butcher to return with the sheep's brains she'd ordered for her dog, Laddie, a long-haired collie just like Lassie. She was planning to put him in the Euroa Dog Show and brains would put an extra shine on his coat. She wasn't prepared for the butcher to return with a whole sheep's head. He placed it on the counter and split the skull with a deft swing of his blade. Lyn watched as its dead staring eyes fell away, the thud, exposing the glistening grey mass that the butcher scooped out with his meaty hands and expertly wrapped in newspaper. She handed over her coins and took all that had been sentient inside the animal in a string bag to feed to her beloved dog.

We weren't brought up on offal, except I do remember once being fed lambs' brains out of a Heinz baby tin and not liking the taste. The little black threads that stood out through the pinky-grey mush reminded me of the black cotton used to stitch me back together after an operation.

At Nana's house in country Euroa, Nana would throw a leg of lamb or side of beef in the oven together with pumpkin and potatoes before we left for Sunday mass. The perfectly cooked meat and roast veggies wrapped in the wood-fired oven made the most delicious lunch, especially with the gravy Nana whisked together from the fatty left-over liquid in the pan.

Nana was tubby with short curly grey hair and she wore pale blue glasses that turned up at the edges like cat's eyes. I liked going out to the woodshed to watch Nana split the logs on the old stump. She was strong. And I sometimes helped her thread the clothes through the manual wringer that sat next to the old copper in her outside laundry. She'd wind the handle and get the two rollers moving with her jobbly arms as I fed in the garments, one by one.

I loved bringing in the split wood and feeding the stove as if it were a ravenous monster with the giant kettle on the stove hissing steam all day. But I didn't love the kidneys or brains mixed in a cheesy white sauce. She cooked the kidneys whole so they were still kidney-shaped. I knew from school that kidneys were the body's filtering system. Imagine eating an organ that absorbed all the yucky stuff in your blood and turned it into pee! It had me wondering how old the poor animal was and how much filtering it had done before it was slaughtered. I had kidneys that very shape in my own body doing the very same thing. What made humans different from animals then, if we had the same sorts of organs in our bodies? Our brains separated us from animals, the teacher said. That, and our opposable thumbs. The brains Nana cooked had black threads through them just like those little lamb brains shoved into a can. I wondered when you ate sheep brains if you were eating all its experiences and memories. I wondered if my brain looked the same. Did the brains settling in my stomach talk to the brain in my skull? It hurt my head just to think about it.

The other thing I had to eat at Nana's was rabbit. The first time I went out past the paddocks with Uncle David I don't think I quite understood what the term 'rabbiting' meant. Uncle David was wiry and good-looking with sharp blue eyes that took in long distances. He took me down to the hutch next to Nana's woodshed under the peppercorn tree. The ferrets were frantic, stinking, liquid-eyed long-bodied creatures. Uncle David scooped a couple into a small wire cage then we went to the back shed, next to the laundry with the old copper, to pick up his rifle.

We followed the trail of rabbit droppings to a network of burrows in the far paddock. Uncle David whispered to keep hush as he lowered the wire cage and let the ferrets out. They ran straight to the burrows and rabbits and little bunnies rushed out. Some froze. Uncle David lifted his rifle and fired. I covered my ears. The first rabbit was a clean shot but the second one screamed, injured and bleeding. Uncle David picked it up and wrung its neck with a twist. I heard the crack and saw it go limp in his hands. I never knew rabbits could make a noise of pure terror like that. I felt tears welling up as Uncle David calmly explained it was the kindest thing to do and you had to do it quickly, with confidence. He gestured a twist with his hands, like a Chinese burn. I imagined someone doing that to my neck and knew, with my bones, it wouldn't take much. I felt numb.

Once Uncle David was finished, there were four rabbits strung up by their back legs on a stick. I walked behind, staring at them slung over his shoulder, swinging like hanged men, wee dribbling down their fur and dripping off their dead, floppy ears.

Uncle David went to the shed to skin and gut them for the pot. I went inside, quietly, inconspicuous, blending in with the noise and scuttle of the house.

'What does rabbit taste like, Mum?' I asked.

'Just like chicken,' she replied.

I was going to ask her if she knew rabbits screamed but I thought she probably did and I knew it wouldn't help in getting that piercing sound out of my head. When the stew was put on the table, I could still see shapes of rabbit among the vegetables. I was starving, so I closed my eyes and dug in. It tasted nothing like chicken.

Two white, pink-eyed rabbits, a boy and a girl, came to live with me. They'd come from the science department at school. I'd been longing for a pet and was never able to have a cat or a dog because I was allergic to them. The rabbits lived in a large metal cage outside, with an enclosed nesting area. I'd cuddle each of them in turn. The girl rabbit dug a deep hole and escaped. The boy rabbit pined for its mate and wouldn't even eat. Mum suggested we take it to Nana's and give it to the Dutch family down the road from her who also had rabbits. With great reluctance, I agreed that it was the kindest thing to do. Rabbits, like humans, need company.

The Dutch family was tough as old boots. They were country people, living on a rambling property with lots of animals and outbuildings. The father was a tall, sinewy man with thick blonde wavy hair and a powerful jaw always set to serious. The mother was broad, ruddy-faced with curly blonde-grey hair. They had at least six children. When there was nothing to do at Nana's, my cousins and I would visit for a change of scenery, even though I was slightly nervous around them.

'Hey, come and get some milk!' One of the Dutch boys called out, squatting on an upturned bucket, his hands pulling on a cow's teats. He leaned forward, sticking the teats upward, sending milk sprays into the air. The other Dutch kids laughed and ran forward, opening their mouths under the arc of the steaming white liquid.

'Go on, get some!' One of them called out and I was pushed from behind. I didn't even like milk unless it had been transformed into cheese or chocolate or ice-cream. My gut lurched. The fluid was thick and warm and tasted like thick cream and cut grass. I gagged and spat it out, watching it trickle in the dirt. They laughed. The city kid couldn't handle it.

The young Dutch teenage daughter complained of a sore neck. Her mother looked at me and laughed.

'Ha, nothing that a lift and a wrench won't fix!'

She put her hands roughly around her daughter's neck and twisted. The daughter began crying.

'Ha!' the mother cried and stomped off.

I stood, staring at the crying girl. I couldn't imagine my mother behaving like that with anyone, let alone her children.

'Are you okay?' I asked feebly.

'Ha!' the girl said and wiped her eyes. 'Come on, I want to show you something.'

She led me to the unused pigsty. Inside, she had me squat down as she pulled back a pile of old flannel and exposed a row of baby mice. Six little pink fingers with tiny limbs, sealed eyes and closed mouths. All dead. I felt queasy looking at their bodies so tiny and helpless. She covered them again and stood up.

'Ha! Too bad,' she said and walked off, leaving me in the broken-down pigsty.

'Shouldn't we bury them?' I called out.

'Nah, just leave 'em,' she called back.

The day I brought my fluffy white-haired, pink-eyed rabbit to live with the Dutch family it took all my strength not to cry. I thought about the mother wrenching her daughter's neck and the dead mice and suddenly felt fearful about leaving my rabbit with them. There were four other rabbits, so at least my bunny would have company, I told myself. They lived in a large hutch built off the ground with lots of straw for bedding and plenty of food scraps. And they were all alive. Everyone stood around while I gave my boy one last cuddle before popping him in with the other rabbits. At least I knew I could have a pat any time I came to visit.

The next day I saw one of the Dutch boys walking up Nana's driveway. He was one of the older kids but he didn't act his age. Short and chubby, his fingers were not properly formed, more like stumps than fingers. I never saw his feet but his misshapen boots had me imagining gnarly toes. He walked with a hobble and I wondered if that's how I looked when I walked. In his hands he held a glass jar half full of slugs. He held them out to me, his fingers resembling the slimy creatures sliding up the glass. The lid was screwed on tight with no air holes.

'How many?' he asked.

'If you want those slugs to live you need to get a nail and punch some holes in the lid,' I said.

He shook his head. 'I got a message,' he said. 'Your rabbit's dead.'

'How? What happened?'

'Dunno. It's dead. I come to tell you.'

He turned and shambled off, swinging his jar of slugs. I learnt later that one of the other male rabbits had killed him. No one had realised that male rabbits were territorial. Rabbits seemed such gentle, cuddly things that I found it difficult to imagine. At night, trammelled with guilt, the scene in my head was a bloody one. My poor white, lonely boy soaked in red, screaming to escape, being savaged to death. Pure terror played and replayed in my head as a punishment for sending him to rabbit hell.

As compensation my Uncle David saved me a wild bunny from his next rabbiting expedition and we brought it home with us. It sat, quivering in its cage and died a couple of weeks later—a tough way to learn that wild rabbits don't survive being caged. Maybe nothing does.

## Auntie's affliction caused by everything and nothing

'Ah, I feel so sorry for that poor little bugger!' Auntie Geraldine said every time I had a joint dislocation or bone break. When she discovered I also had the same allergic itchy-skin problems she did, she kindly sent me a bottle of her 'liquid gold'. It smelled like old compost. I dribbled the silky solution, cool and pungent, onto my skin. A few days later the top layer of skin cracked and peeled then fell away and underneath everything was a tender baby pink.

Auntie Geraldine had been slapping coal tar on her burning skin for years but, unlike me, she had been perfectly healthy until she turned seventeen. Suddenly, without explanation, Geraldine was struck down with nobody-knew-what. Her beautiful complexion was replaced with a scourge of red irritation overnight and from that point on she scratched her way into a kind of madness. I knew she had been beautiful because I'd seen a photo of her looking like Judy Garland in *The Wizard of Oz* with her long auburn hair parted in the middle and two plaits draped over her shoulders. No doctor could pinpoint a cause or solution. The coal tar was brutal. She shed like a snake but it was the only thing that gave her temporary relief. Refreshed layers held hope of a new beginning.

By the time I was a teenager, Auntie Geraldine had begun losing her eyesight. Her eyeballs had become as irritated as her skin. Each inflammation left scars and each scar appeared as a blot on her vision.

'Jeez, it's like seeing the world through a dirty sponge with only a few pin holes in it!' she cried in her dry, throaty voice.

Auntie Geraldine, Uncle Bernie and my cousins lived in the northern suburbs of Melbourne until the family had saved enough to buy a bush block in Wandong just out of Kilmore. Auntie and Uncle lived in a galvanised shed with my youngest cousin until their wooden kit home had enough rooms for visitors.

'Lovely to see ya!' Auntie Geraldine croaked as she picked her way gingerly over the rough ground towards our car. Her face and arms were dry and blotchy, her red hair short and grey at the roots.

Auntie proudly showed us around, talking loudly out of the side of her mouth telling us what Uncle still needed to do. She also told us her last allergy tests revealed an immune system so dysfunctional she was allergic to almost everything—foods of all kinds, dust, pollens, animals, mud.

'But do ya know the thing I'm most allergic to?' she asked, throwing me a wink.

'No,' I said.

'Your Uncle Bernie!' she cackled. 'I don't think we can share the same bed anymore; he's making me sick.'

'Geraldine! The children!' Mum squeaked, unable to hide a smirk.

Meanwhile Dad and Uncle were deep in discussion in the lounge-cum-kitchen-cum-dining room. Uncle had been showing Dad how he'd been sitting nightly by the lamp and hand sewing a sheepskin into a coat. He'd managed to finish one side. It would go with his Akubra. He was also trying to fix a string on his guitar and was talking like a musical pro until Auntie led us into the room and interrupted his soliloquy.

'Aw, come on Bernie, you can only play one song. What's it called again? *Tumblin' Tumbleweeds*, that's it. Sings it best if he's chewin' on a piece of hay,' she said, rolling her bloodshot eyes in our direction.

My cousin, brother and sisters had gone to play outside but being the eldest, I stuck with Mum and Auntie Geraldine.

'Come and I'll show you my Mary,' she said.

'Who's Mary?' I asked.

'Well, she gets me through the day,' Auntie replied, looking past the house to the dense bushland beyond. 'And she's living in God's backyard.'

'You stay here and mind the kids,' Mum said to me, and they walked off, arm in arm, beyond the clearing. I stood there a while until a strange, sweet-smelling smoke wafted from the trees, tickling my nostrils.

Mary's surname was 'Juana'.

A couple of hours before dusk, Dad started up the car. He didn't want to be hitting roos on the way home. Auntie Geraldine warned us to look out for the wired stakes that mapped out the rest of the house, yet to be built.

'Now watch you don't drive through the laundry!' she cackled, waving us off.

The last time I saw Auntie Geraldine her short, dyed red hair had grown long and grey and was plaited in one long coil down her back. Her face was pale, serene. Her eyes, from which she could barely see, looked distant. She moved slowly, like a sanctimonious nun. I wanted her to say something brash like, 'I'm so hungry I could eat a baby's bum through the bottom of a cane chair!' at the top of her voice but she barely spoke.

My itchiness was intermittent but Auntie's had been never-ending. Her body had fashioned its own circuit-breaker. Her brain had formed a mass at its stem, calming the central nervous system, releasing her from the torment that might have sent a less resilient person over a cliff. Death came a few months later in a hospital bed surrounded by my mother and all her siblings.

'Let go, big sister, let go,' they whispered.

# TAKING CONTROL

## Go forth, rebel!

As a rare specimen, I had magnetic qualities that attracted an array of doctors who sometimes forgot I was of the same species. The rude ones had implacable stares and assumed I had the intelligence of a lesser animal. The polite ones requested my permission to do certain things but still treated me as if I were a lab rat. All were men.

One of the most traumatic experiences was being examined in an auditorium full of men in white coats when I was nine years old. I had to walk the length of the auditorium naked except for a singlet that just covered my bottom. If I'd been any closer to adolescence, I'm sure I would have flatly refused. Our family didn't walk around naked at home. We weren't that sort of family. I did still share baths with my brother four years younger than me, but that was different. These people were strangers. However, Mum convinced me I was sacrificing very little if it meant the specialists could learn something from me to help other kids like me.

I was the only female—a girl—in a sea of doctors, most of them peering through spectacles like magnifying glasses. They all leaned towards me as I walked in between rows, a naked Bride of Christ before the altar, my eyes scanning forward and down as I was told by the professor at the front to 'stop', 'walk back', 'turn', 'stop', 'walk ahead'. It was a nightmare of 'I've-suddenly-found-myself-naked-in-public' proportions. I felt my face heating up and felt even more exposed. Everyone could see my feelings, my embarrassment. The professor gave a commentary as I went. I was a walking miracle, expected not to be able to walk at all. Some people might say I was brave, but I moved my body just as all bodies want to move. When I was younger, I didn't know I wasn't meant to get about the way I did. I just got on with it.

The professor finally asked me to stop in front of him. His assistant, lifting me up on to a white table with my back to the sea of white coats whispered, 'I'm just going to lift your singlet up for a brief moment so we can observe your hips.'

Mum had prepped me for this moment, but those few seconds of everyone seeing my bum still made me almost faint.

When I was smaller, I asked Mum how fast a second was. She said it was the fastest piece of time. I recalled jumping on the spot, trying to make the fastest jump I could because then it would be a second. The fastest second. But those few seconds standing on that white table with my back to everyone felt like the longest piece of time. I was taken down off the table and I think a dressing gown was draped over me. Not that it mattered by then.

As I grew towards puberty and became more self-conscious about my body the medical interactions became even more awkward. Not long after I'd first developed breasts, I was in a doctor's surgery being asked to take deep breaths while a stethoscope lay cold on my chest. I was susceptible to bronchitis and pneumonia as well as seasonal asthma. There were two doctors there that day. The one checking my breathing was a student doctor. As he moved the stethoscope around, sliding this way and that beneath my unbuttoned shirt, I blurted out, 'I have a weak chest.' A smirk crept over his face as he looked across to the doctor in charge and said with a knowing smirk, 'Oh, your chest looks pretty good to me!' Both of them smiled, looking at each other then back to me, as if what had just been said was a compliment. I swallowed and looked away, suddenly embarrassed and confused. Weren't adults in positions of authority more responsible than this? Did I hear right? Ultimately, I blamed myself for saying something that was clearly stupid.

No wonder I became so self-conscious as a young adolescent that I went through a period of blushing at the tiniest, even imaginary, acknowledgement of my body. I mumbled when spoken to, afraid I might say something wrong or inappropriate. Interactions were painful. I wanted to be nothing more than an invisible observer. Anyone's gaze in my direction, however fleeting, became a piercing X-ray. I felt raw, naked to my soul.

At fifteen I developed severe pneumonia for the umpteenth time. An ambulance took me to emergency where I struggled for breath, waiting for the X-ray, the diagnosis, the prognosis, the antibiotics. Three medicos came to me with a rubber hammer— clearly not an instrument with which to examine my rattling chest. They hit the tendons below my kneecaps. One knee flexed at a slightly different angle to the other. They were as fascinated as children discovering the workings of a novelty toy. I fought to stay calm, to breathe shallow, steady breaths. They kept looking at my knees as I watched, glassy-eyed and feverish. I appreciate that doctors can be fascinated when they come across someone with a rare condition they may have read about in medical books but not seen in a patient in captivity. As they went on talking amongst themselves about how novel my body was, I threw my head back and with the little oxygen left in my infected lungs screamed, 'Fuck off!! All of you just FUCK OFF!!'

They backed off, speechless. The specimen had spoken.

## A top-heavy tertiary learning curve

I began uni in the early 1980s and by then my naturally large breasts were causing increasing back, neck and shoulder pain. I was still walking on dislocated hips. I was too young for hip replacements. Prosthetic hips would only last a maximum of ten years before I'd require a revision and there's a limit to how many revisions anyone can have and, at any rate, there was not enough bone mass in my pelvis to sustain such a surgery. I would have cracked like an egg. I was 'inoperable'.

Out of desperation I contacted the orthopaedic surgeon who had looked after me when I was a child. He took my call but as soon as I began crying about the pain I was in, he couldn't wait to get off the phone.

I was excited to be at uni. I'd chosen to do a Bachelor of Education not because I wanted to be a teacher necessarily but because I could study creative arts—music, media and drama—and have the back-up of teaching if nothing else panned out. I loved being around other creative people but it was hard to enjoy anything when I could barely think from the pain.

Yasmin, a mature-aged student with a beautiful jazz voice, performed in her own band. To me she was sophisticated and exotic with her perfumed oils and Indian headscarves. Hippies hadn't featured much in my outer-urban upbringing and the uni students just out of high school, which was most of us, tended to swing culturally between post-punk nihilism and new romanticism. We were the hippy-hangover era trying to find our feet in a post-Vietnam post-Whitlam Fraser 'razor gang' world.

Yasmin told me of this 'amazing' friend of hers who practised alternative therapies and she thought he might be able to help me. I was ready to try anything.

I took the tram to an unremarkable side street, walked to an unremarkable building, rang the bell and was immediately face-to-face with Yasmin's friend: a skinny, middle-aged, man with long hair tied back in a ponytail wearing cheesecloth pants. I explained what was giving me grief and he asked me to get onto his examination table. He felt the crooked skeleton beneath my overwrought muscles then, demonstrating with a stack of polystyrene cups, proceeded to mansplain my crooked spine.

'This is what a correctly postured spine looks like,' he said, holding the cups more or less straight up. 'And this is a spine not properly aligned, like yours,' he said, moving them into a double curvature. I was 'out of balance' and this was causing all my problems. No shit, Sherlock. The simple solution, he said, was to line up my vertebrae into a 'normal' position and this was possible with a simple chiropractic manipulation.

I sprang from the table before he could touch me and woman-splained how and why this was NOT a good idea. Nothing, least of all a chiro job, was going to straighten my back while all my foundations were crooked. Startled by my rejection he took a step back, paused, and told me to wait one moment before disappearing into a back room. He returned with a brown bottle with a white label on which he'd hastily scrawled 'xray'. This was my parting gift, a homeopathic remedy that would apparently take away all the accumulative effects of the numerous X-rays I'd been subjected to. I took a few drops under my tongue as instructed. Water laced with brandy. On the tram ride home I guzzled the lot and made a note to pick up some spirits next time I went shopping.

Not long after, I was getting up from studying on the floor when both my kneecaps fully dislocated. The left patella had done this before but for some reason this time my right patella joined in. I collapsed on my stomach from the pain but managed to grab the metal leg of a bookcase to pull myself forward. This put both patellas back into position but after that I lay motionless too scared to move. I was living with my aunt Claire in Carlton at the time and my screams had her rushing downstairs. She gave me Panadol and put packs of frozen vegetables over my knees to ease the swelling. I settled on the floor in a makeshift bed. If I moved, with my knees fat and swollen as they were, I was at risk of dislocating them again. I spent the week at home writing essays on the floor, sniffing amyl nitrate and feeling sorry for myself.

I was so shaken by both knees giving way I took to wearing knee braces under my jeans. My greatest fear was to collapse in public, especially when acting on stage. I'd even auditioned and got a part as Miss Prism in an extra-curricular production of *The Importance of Being Earnest*. Once I'd costumed up in my high-necked blouse, stockings, petticoat and floor-length skirt, I snuck into the toilets and dragged the thick elastic braces over my knees. The stage, made up of rickety rostrums, had me sweating every time I walked out under the lights. And my fears weren't unrealistic. One night, when the large bosomy woman playing Lady Bracknell thumped her way on stage, the rostrum shifted and she slipped. In a spontaneous addition to Oscar Wilde's script, she declared, 'One seemed to have not attended to proper repairs following the earthquake of 1899!'

I survived the play and gradually became confident on my legs again but I was still stuck with all the upper body pain. Short of any other solution, I began to consider a breast reduction. Mum suggested I go to the family GP, a good Catholic family man with a tribe of children, who had delivered all Mum's babies except me.

After asking about the rest of the family he told me to get up on the examination table and remove my top. As I began following his instructions, he told me I'd turned into quite an attractive young woman and asked if I had a boyfriend. My guts churned. I felt trapped as if it were a trick question. I stared him straight in the eye and said 'No.' It wasn't a lie, I was in a relationship with my first girlfriend. I wasn't here to talk to him about my love life. I just wanted to be referred to a specialist about a breast reduction.

I sat there, self-conscious, as he took a breast in each hand and, jiggling them, said, 'Any operation is risky and this would be an unnecessary one. Some man's going to love these one day.'

The surgeon I was finally referred to for breast surgery was a paunchy old man who operated out of a private hospital. He understood why I wanted a reduction and went on to explain I would be left with scars, possible numbness and blocked milk ducts. Aside from numbness the rest wasn't up for consideration. What were more scars? And I had enough trouble looking after myself let alone producing a child that statistically had a 50% chance of inheriting my genetic condition.

The paunchy breast surgeon opened a desk drawer and pulled out a series of polaroids with 'before' and 'after' photos. There were no heads, just topless torsos he'd operated on. Sifting through the photos that de-identified and objectified these women felt creepy. I had to assume they'd been happy with the results but found it hard to separate the medical pragmatics from the suggestive, almost pornographic violence of it all.

Now it was my turn. He told me to strip off as he picked up the polaroid instant camera and took my 'before' shots. He then felt my breasts, comparing the size of each and showing me where he would be cutting. I would have been far more comfortable with a woman supervising—a nurse perhaps—but at least this felt more of a clinical exercise than my experience with the Catholic GP. I couldn't help feeling like a piece of meat. We talked about size. He said he'd leave me 'a decent handful'. Would a female surgeon have spoken to me like that?

This was the first time I'd struck out on my own, initiating a medical procedure. I lay in the hospital bed, my pillow soaked with tears. I held on to my breasts and mourned them as if they were soft animals I was sending off to be slaughtered.

I lay there remembering every other one of my operations and medical interventions. The fear of losing bodily autonomy, of something going wrong, of the physical pain. All that built a tsunami of fear.

I woke with the familiar stinging post-operative sensation across my chest wall and the heavy weight of a tightly wound pressure bandage. Grief and relief wavered through my foggy brain as the pain arced and I pressed the bell for my first post-operative dose of painkillers. I imagined my cut-off bits lying in a kidney-shaped tray waiting to be incinerated.

I returned to the surgeon's consulting rooms for my 'after' photo. Everything 'looked perky' and the surgeon added my polaroid to the pile.

As the pain eased and the scars healed I felt so light I was almost giddy. I no longer needed to wear fulsome underwire bras. Sometimes I didn't wear a bra at all. I was finally in proportion, thin and even-breasted and ready to move a little easier through the world.

# WILD AND TERRIBLE

## (And the spaces between)

### Other lands—one: from tropics to snowfall

1986. I was twenty-five years old and desperate for adventure. My biological clock was ticking not for a child but for a chance to travel before I estimated I'd be getting about in a wheelchair. And I wanted to walk about the world while I had the chance. Instinct told me I had about ten years. At this point no surgeon would operate on me so instinct was my best bet. I began to save and dream of overseas destinations. How much of the world could I drink in? I was so thirsty.

I worked in various art programs at the City of Caulfield, lived in an apartment in East St Kilda and bought a bike so I could get fit. I bought a backpack and practised carrying an increasing weight of belongings. Trolley cases had yet to be invented so I had no choice but to carry my belongings this way. Once I had enough saved, I bought a one-way ticket to Japan and told everyone my plans were—indefinite! Infinite! Some considered me irresponsible. I considered it a necessary call of the wild.

A foreign land puts every sense on high alert. The newness, the excitement of living in a constant state of hyper-vigilance is like continuous shots of caffeine hitting the bloodstream. Being a young female with a physical disability added an extra edge.

1987. New Year's Eve. Bali hit me with a great wall of humidity, blinding verdant green and bare blue sky. Overwhelmed by fighting cocks, street sellers, motorbikes and cow bells, I was shocked that a laid-back tropical paradise could be noisier than an inner Melbourne suburb. The smell of clove cigarettes settled at the back of my nostrils, mixed with sizzling street food and ripe tropical fruit.

More than once, my backpack, heavy with belongings, managed to pull me backwards onto the ground like an upturned beetle. My body strained in this place designed for relaxation as my tanning skin belied knotted muscles and aching joints. I lounged on the beach in a cheap sarong that imprinted my sweaty skin with orange, red and gold. Lying face down on my towel, I accepted a massage from a couple of local women but, being rubbed with oil mixed with sand on sunburned skin as other vendors took advantage by simultaneously trying to sell me silver jewellery and wooden carvings, was hardly therapeutic. I may have saved for over a year to afford this trip but, to the Balinese, all tourists had wads of money to spend. The fact that I could afford to visit was proof enough of wealth and I had no baseline from which to barter. I simply paid them enough so they'd leave me alone.

After that experience I decided on observation over participation. I avoided sexual harassment by eyeing off people from behind a book. I avoided Bali Belly by drinking from freshly unsealed bottles, and refusing street food and cooked meat. I watched locals walking with full baskets on their heads or begging on roadsides. Skinny and diseased street dogs sniffed for scraps in the dust. Wildly carefree tourists wove in and out of bars and nightclubs, drunk on booze and freedom from whatever waited for them back home.

Two weeks later I was north of the equator freezing my tits off.

Tokyo hit me with an icy blast at minus ten degrees Celsius. I rode a bicycle in the snow and caught snowflakes on my tongue.

I took a bullet train to the mountains and stayed in a traditional home with tatami mats and rice paper screens. I went to public baths and scrubbed my skin pink and sank into pools so hot it was painful to move. I climbed a thousand temple steps until my hips could take no more, but I was so elated I didn't care.

In Hiroshima I saw remnants of buildings twisted by the atomic bomb. There was no grass in the nearby Peace Park and I wondered if it was because the radioactive fallout had sterilised the ground.

I watched enormous sumo wrestlers battle it out in a circle of sand and wondered what this did to their bodies. I was told most wrestlers didn't live beyond the age of fifty. Obesity, brute strength and a guaranteed short life afforded them the godlike status of Buddha-shaped pop stars.

I stayed and got a job teaching English to businessmen, children and housewives. One day, in a classroom on the fourteenth floor, the building began swaying back and forth as the floor thumped like a beating heart. I found myself on my knees, crying, 'Stop! Just STOP!' The students stared at me inscrutably and quietly slipped under the tables until the earth stopped moving. I was too terrified to feel foolish.

The next substantial earthquake occurred while I was in Tokyo's underground rail network. The train stopped and we were thrown into darkness. My carriage was full of commuters but there was complete silence, not even a muffled cough. I imagined being crushed and buried with all these strangers and, even if we survived the initial impact, our bodies would never be retrieved and we would slowly suffocate as we sucked in what was left of the oxygen in that cylindrical concrete tomb.

I don't know how people live in a city that records up to twenty tremors a day knowing that the BIG one, now overdue, could swallow the city whole at any moment. My anxiety was constant and often overwhelming.

By the time I boarded a flight home to Melbourne, my right leg without a hip socket had become a few centimetres shorter and the glands in my throat had become swollen. It took me months to be diagnosed with Chronic Fatigue Syndrome (CFS), which continued to haunt me for years. But I never regretted my year-long Japanese adventure. Maybe I would have developed CFS and a deteriorating hip whether I'd travelled overseas or not. My only regret was not being able to take that slow boat to China and trek across Europe with an Irish woman I'd met. Instead, I had to return home and deal with my painful, useless hip and Chronic Fatigue.


## Gaining traction—one: a cluster of clowns

1989. I was exhausted. I looked terrible. All in the mind, the doctors said. They barely acknowledged that something like CFS even existed, let alone was treatable. I spent money I'd earned in Japan working through every alternative therapy trying to find the one thing that could give me relief from feeling so ill that I could barely lift my head off a pillow. My brain was so foggy I couldn't focus on the most mundane TV show, let alone read. My right leg had become so much shorter than my left leg that I could only walk with a raised foot—just as I'd done as a baby learning to stand in my cot.

I eventually collapsed in pain on my lounge room floor. It was my twenty-eighth birthday and I waited six unbearable hours for the ambulance to arrive. I was sure I'd done some sort of irreparable damage but, when I eventually arrived at emergency, I was told that the muscles around my lower back, pelvis and hips had simply gone into extreme spasm in a vain attempt to hold all my crookedness together.

Both legs bound from the knees down, weights tugging them over the end of the bed. I'm in a public hospital with an orthopaedic surgeon who doesn't know what to do with me. He doesn't want to operate on my hips because he says he can't guarantee a good result. Instead, he puts both legs in traction, ordering the nurses to gradually increase the weights on the pulley to release the pressure on my hips, especially the right hip that, over the last twelve months, has gradually worked its way further into my buttocks.

This is the too-hard-basket ward—the ward furthest away from the nurses' station. Patients come and go but the young woman in the bed opposite me is going nowhere. She has some rare disease that is numbing and wasting her body from the feet up. It has reached her navel. She barely gets out of bed and, when she does, she has to drag her upper body across and grab her legs to make them follow. She's not a light person and it is a great struggle. Meanwhile I lie strapped, unable to turn or move.

We are both in our twenties. We are meant to have futures. At home, she lives in a room at the back of her parent's house but her family is finding it increasingly difficult to attend to her needs. We are the 'degeneratives' without medical solutions, without a medical routine, except for a laxative or a painkiller, waiting for morning washes, breakfast, morning tea, lunch, afternoon tea, dinner. There's nothing to be done. TV and magazines pass only so much of the day. She remains insanely cheery with the nurses but slumps into silence once they leave. The only thing that perks me up is feeling sorrier for her than myself. She and I both know she's probably going to end up in a nursing home with a bunch of people her grandmother's age. Where does that put me? The pit of hopelessness lies just below the hospital's shiny surfaces.

A couple of friends visit me. They have been making a film about clowns. They try to cheer me up with silly routines—a plastic ice-cream cone with a ball of sponge shoots off and flies at me. I struggle to laugh, a double act of sad clowndom. Not even a clown doctor would want to visit this ward.

I have flutters of panic locked in this holding pattern. Whatever is being done to me is temporary at best but I am told a hip replacement is so very risky. My pelvis is so thin there is not enough bone mass to create a socket where there has never been one. The only other suggestion has been to fuse my hip joints to minimise the grinding pain. A fused hip cannot move. I had two options: did I want my hips set in a standing position or at ninety degrees for a sitting position? Either way it would be permanent. I think of the girl in the other bed and wonder if we'd both be better ordering amputations.

The food trolley comes last to our ward-at-the-end-of-all-wards. I've always liked toast for breakfast. Sometimes I even risk ordering it in hospital. I savour hot toast with melting butter and honey. To stave off delivering cold, hard toasted bread the kitchen has started placing the toast on polystyrene squares. This might have kept things warm for patients five minutes from the kitchen but by the time it reaches us the toast has sweated into the thermoplastic polymer, sodden underneath and cold on top. Before the food trays are collected, I write on the polystyrene plate with pen: THIS IS AN ENVIRONMENTAL NIGHT-MARE! I order toast for the next week just to get my message across. The hospital stops using the polystyrene though I expect it's not because of my environmental activism but because the material has failed to keep toast hot or edible.

A nurse bustles in and says the surgeon has ordered the weights to be taken off. She goes to the end of the bed, lifts everything away and walks out the door. The traction that had been gradually weighted over a couple of weeks, pulling the joints and tendons away from each other is suddenly gone. I feel like the Wicked Witch of the West in the *Wizard of Oz* whose legs recoil after Dorothy's house has landed on her. My muscles and tendons spring back in an opposite trajectory to a bungy jump.

Hot knives dance round my groin. I cry quietly. I buzz for a nurse. I cry noisily. I buzz again. A nurse comes to the doorway.

'They took it all off. Too much. All off!'

The nurse darts away. The woman opposite buzzes too, hoping the double alarm will get someone back who'll do something. Finally, the nurse-in-charge arrives and pulls a chair up to my bed. She hands me water and some pain pills and tries to calm me down. She looks worried but I can tell she isn't worried for my sake; she wants me to shut up. She has the look of a child who's gone too far with her younger sibling and doesn't want the parents to find out. It doesn't take a genius to work out that if the weights had been added gradually over a number of days, then they should have been removed in the same manner. I'm now in more pain than I'd been in when I first arrived. I take all the pain relief they will give me and discharge myself. I must keep looking for a surgeon who can do something I can live with or find a way to disappear.

## Me? I'm a chemical princess

1990. The first bone and tissue bank in Australasia established in 1989, the Donor Tissue Bank of Victoria, received deposits from both the living and the dead. Unlike organs, bone can be stored for long periods and is not rejected by the body. Portions can be carved to any shape and grafted onto bone that's eventually absorbed into the recipient's genetic material. Not ideal for someone like me with faulty bone genetics but at least there was the potential to add bone mass where I had little. I looked to the Donor Tissue Bank of Victoria as my potential saviour— the answer to receiving a new metal hip.

However, the orthopaedic fraternity was almost unanimous in its rejection of the idea of a hip replacement. They would consider people in their seventies and above only. A prosthetic hip would be lucky to last ten years but, for me, the prospect of a failed hip a decade down the track was surely better than no future at all.

Surgeon after surgeon refused to operate but, eventually, I found a senior professor who'd had recent success with a young woman in similar circumstances to mine. It would involve adding donor bone to create a hip socket that could house a prosthetic joint. Ironically, the donor bone would be coming from me. The ball of my femur, which must be sliced off to insert the prosthesis, would be used to create a properly formed hip socket. He warned it was high risk. There was a litany of things that could go wrong, including a failed bone graft, but I just had to hope the odds were on my side.

The narrow room is sickly yellow, fluorescent, lined with plastic trays and tubes and needles and rubber gloves. The nurse has given me something to make me relax but my pulse keeps twitching. I feel foolish, lying here in a too-big hospital gown with no underpants and a hairnet that does nothing to contain my curls. My breath flutters and I hold it, attempting to stop time and everything else.

How do you wait to be knocked out and cut open?

A doctor elbows through the swing door, his gloved hands held up to avoid touching anything. He has a blue surgical mask over his face and a white cotton head covering tied at the back. I try not to look beyond the door. It's where I'm going to be any minute now. I can't hear what the doctor says through his mask, so I just stare at him. It's cold in this room and I only have a white sheet and a cotton blanket covering me. Nothing is tucked in, not even the back of my hospital gown. I imagine he sees me as pale, my nose and lips a bluish tinge, all pinched in—a frozen bird. The air in the operating room beyond the swing door is even colder to freeze out germs. I don't know how the nurses and doctors keep warm. Perhaps they do star jumps in between the slicing and chopping and everything else they do with all those shiny metal tools all lined up on a shiny metal tray. It always scares me that I won't be quite asleep when they take up the scalpel— or I'll wake up in the middle but won't be able to open my eyes or scream and I'll just feel the pain.

They trolley me through the swing door. My insides jump and twist. I could be going down a fast lift or being pushed high on a swing but no, the side rails of the trolley are being pulled down, they are pushing a cold plastic slide under me and voomph! I'm on the operating table, staring at a bright sun hung on a metal arm. There's no going back. There are people around me and the black mask is coming over my mouth. 'Count backwards from ten,' a white-clad someone says. But I do it my way. I close my eyes and keep looking. It's like rushing into a train tunnel. Whoosh! I count from one to ten, imagining each count a second in time. How long will I last? I rush through the tunnel and the last thing I feel is the sense of falling from a tall building. Then, moments before hitting the ground, there's a rushing in my ears and a pinwheel of colours against the black. Then dreamless nothing.

My eyes open in the recovery room and, as always, I am far too alert. I dare not move, not even to twist my head, before I do a reconnoitre of muscle, bone, tendon. Yes, I can feel where I've been sawn open and stitched up. It's a deep, stinging pain despite the medication pumping into my veins, into my blood, swirling through all my inside tunnels like a waterslide. It is post-operative pain. Before surgery the pain is deep, gnawing, and unrelenting. After surgery the strong, stinging sensation feels like a million cells rushing to seal the slice, to bind metal to bone and screws to metal.

I hear groaning from the bed to the left of me. The boy is connected, as I am, to drips and monitoring equipment that flash and beep as if we are in an aviary with dozens of twittering, flapping monotonous robot birds. The boy is trying to sit up. He is pulling at the tubes in his arms. He's working to pull off the oxygen mask. I know it's suffocating to wake up with that plastic thing covering your nose and mouth. The hissing steam of something you feel your lungs can't take in but has you feeling worse if you don't. A nurse runs to the boy's side and tries to get him to lie back against the pillow but he's having none of it. Another nurse runs to assist, then another. It's not until he's injected with something that he gives up and flakes out again I must look a bit disturbed because one of the nurses comes over and explains that some people wake up from anaesthetic all groggy and disoriented. They don't understand where they are and why they're stuck in a bed with all the tubes and machines. So, this boy is not being disruptive on purpose, it's something out of his control. When I come out of anaesthetic, I feel more awake than before I was put to sleep. I never feel sick. As soon as I can speak, I ask for food but of course you can't have anything to eat so soon after an operation. It's always ice-cubes to suck on, or little sips of water, or if you're really lucky, a lemonade icy pole. A woman further away retches and vomits in her bed. Some people just can't take it. Me, I'm a chemical princess. The only things I have a bad reaction to are natural things, like horses and cats and dogs and grass pollen.

When can I go back to the ward and have a sandwich? Operation's done. What's next? 'Whoa,' says the surgeon, who's come to my bed. 'You've got a lot of resting to do. While you've been asleep your body has been around the world six times.'

### Gaining traction—two: from a Picasso to a Matisse

I lay in my single room on the seventh floor next to a large sealed, sky-filled window. The operation had been successful, transforming me from a Picasso to a Matisse; my right leg had been rotated ninety-five degrees, pulled down five centimetres, the ball of my femur saved from the bin to graft a socket where none had been. My right thigh muscle spasmed wildly in protest.

I was lashed to the bed in traction with a figure eight bandage from ankle to knee. This bandage had to be reconfigured once a day. It took two nurses: one to pull against my leg and one to unwrap and rework the criss-crossing so it was firm yet a little giving. Most nurses, it seemed, had little practice in figure eight dressings. I lost count of how many times the bandage slipped and bunched round my ankle or loosened itself into irrelevance.

The nurses got sick of my 'complaining'. I lay there, knowing this whole transformation was touch and go. So much could still go wrong. If the traction wasn't holding then I didn't want to imagine how my grafted hip socket or the shaft hammered into my femur or the metal ball capped in plastic were faring. I was at everyone's mercy lying here on my back, unable to turn or move for the duration. I needed things to go right. I swallowed my apprehension, waited until the most sensible nurse-in-charge was on duty and told her that every nurse who was going to attend to me needed to know, with confidence, how to wrap a figure eight bandage. If she was a little put out, I had visible proof—the traction bandage was wrapped clumsily round and round my calf without a figure eight in sight. Two days later, six nurses stood round my bed and had figure-eight-bandage training.

A couple of weeks into this improved routine I was feeling more pain than I should have. Regular pulse checks showed my heart was beating too fast. A slight anomaly, a curiosity recorded on my chart. Stuck as I was in the bed, I required bedpans. I had to raise myself, placing my hands in the triangle hanging from the chain over my bed—the monkey bar—long enough for the pan to be slipped under. I could only wear a nightie or pyjama top; there was no way to put bottom halves on and off when in traction. Each time the effort became more excruciating. I instinctively began to grab onto the traction ropes to minimise the movement of my leg as the bedpan was slipped under. A no-fuss nurse saw what I was doing and tried to prise my hand away from the ropes. I fought against her, white knuckled. She called me a sook. She told me I had to let go, it was counter to what had to be done. She finally succeeded in pulling my hand away, simultaneously sliding the pan beneath me. I let out an almighty bellow that blanched her suntanned face. I couldn't bear the pan beneath me. She pulled it away and I was left to catch my breath, afraid of wetting the bed and the sheet shuffling disturbance that would entail.

An X-ray was ordered. The metal shaft that had been hammered into my femur had splintered the bone so that every time I was moved the fracture moved with me, splitting it ever wider. My medical chart was checked and the graph of my quickening pulse, my overworked heart, reflected the distress my body had been in for days. I was whisked back into surgery and sliced open a second time to wire me up. That the surgery was a form of carpentry was apparent in those post-operative X-rays showing the bands of wire wrapped round the fracture point. I was a small adult, barely 150 centimetres tall and around 50 kilograms, and the smallest adult-sized prosthesis at the time was larger than my small bones could accommodate. This is why the fracture had occurred. The wires held however, and the healing began.

The nurse whose eardrum I almost shattered started coming into my room more often than necessary. She made sure the food tray on the trolley was close enough for me to access. She danced to the cassettes I played quietly on my ghetto blaster. I was obsessed with *The Sundays*, their sweeping rhythms and Harriet Wheeler's sweet, soaring voice. The nurse asked me if I'd heard of a band called *Bluehouse*. She rubbed my feet when they were cold and went so far as to buy me extra warm bed socks. She declared I was too tiny-thin. I had no arse, she said. Another nurse came in and whispered, with a laugh, that this nurse had a crush on me.

'No shit, Sherlock!' I said.

A new nurse began nightshift. I think he was from a nurse bank, not a regular. He sidled over to my bedside and grabbed my Body Shop lip balm, twisting off the lid and dipping his little finger in as he asked me if he could have some, smearing it across his lips before I had chance to open my mouth. I felt violated, my lip balm sullied with what I imagined to be an unhygienic digit. He slid onto the bed close to my face, smacked his lips together and grinned as if we'd just shared an intimate moment. I stared at him, my body too heavily medicated to respond verbally. Then he was off with a wave and a promise he would be back later.

I stirred in my sleep. I felt some movement at the end of the bed and was woken by a torch breaking the darkness. It was Mr Lip Balm.

'What?' I muttered, half asleep.

'Just checking in … go back to sleep,' he whispered.

The torch went dead as he closed the door. I lay in the dark, feeling uneasy. Hospital bedding cannot be tucked in at the bottom if there's traction in the way. I had one leg stretched, hanging out of the bed and no underwear on. What was he checking on, exactly? I imagined the worst and wished myself awake for the rest of the night, fighting off the medication that had my eyes drooping, my body floating in a weightless world in the dark. As the light rose through my sealed window, I told myself nothing had happened, though every cell told me otherwise. What could I say? What to tell? A nurse used my lip balm? I told the nurse-in-charge I didn't feel comfortable with him and I wouldn't sleep knowing he was on night duty. I never saw him again. Perhaps I hadn't been the only one who'd felt their creep-o-meter rise when he entered the room.

The complication with the fracture translated to nine weeks in traction—over two months of never turning on my side, lying on my front, sitting up, bending my leg. It takes a certain type of thinking not to fall into a disturbed state of mind stuck in such a predicament. I imagined my mind was a little cricket in a matchbox, aware but hibernating, slow breathing, stilling runaway thoughts.

My body wasn't normal but it craved normality. Bodies are designed to move. I wasn't exactly in solitary confinement but I only ever left my room, though not my bed, to have an X-ray. I spent many hours alone. Nurses were busy. Kitchen staff were run off their feet. Cleaners made so much noise with their vacuums and polishing machines there was no opportunity for banter. Visitors came and went but as the time went on it was natural for people to fall away. Mum visited when she could but she had to travel a long distance. Halfway through my stay she arrived with my teddy bear, Samuel. I'd been given Samuel by one of my father's friends when I was three weeks old. Mum tucked Samuel in beside me before she left. Something inside me broke. I clutched Samuel and cried, then howled. I felt tears soaking the pillow, my hair, my ears. I cried for my father, six years dead. I cried like a baby swaddled in a cot crying for its mother. I cried for the loneliness of my circumstance. I cried for not being able to dance, to party, to celebrate anything, anything at all. I cried for loss of hope. I cried 'til every one of my molecules tingled with a strange energy. By the time a nurse arrived I was hyperventilating. The imbalance of oxygen and carbon dioxide in my lungs had a strangely calming effect. I felt lifted out of myself. It was an escape like no other, the post-operative pain suddenly suppressed by what felt like a multi-cellular vibration, a consortium of microwaves sending me away, away, ethereal, reconstituted. I didn't want the sensation to stop. The cricket had sprung from its matchbox, alert, rasping, ready for flight.

## Mr Tough Guy by the peppercorn tree

The peppercorn tree is my refuge, a little scrap of nature in a court-yard of concrete and pebbles. I like to crush its leaves between my palms and inhale its pungency. It reminds me of the old peppercorn at the bottom of my grandmother's garden behind the woodshed and next to the cage where Uncle David kept his smelly ferrets. The old patients only come here when they're wheeled out by relatives desperate for fresh air and a smoke. The young ones stay on their balconies where it's easier to drink smuggled alcohol. Me? I have a small bottle of Scotch hidden in the cupboard below my locked drugs drawer full of stuff incompatible with alcohol: contraindicational, the lot of them. I know staff sometimes smell it on my breath. I can see it in their eyes and my eyes tell them I dare you. It's been a silent stand off so far.

Rehab smells of soiled bandages and stale urine. The room, on one of the top floors of the hospital, is bright with fluorescence. The orderly has wheeled me to my favourite spot where I can see a piece of sky. I imagine the fragrance of grass. The best way to survive here is to look outward. It's a dizzying experience pressing one's nose against the sealed glass, looking down to the street and to the top of the trees that, from such a height, are mere shrubs. I imagine falling through the pane and wonder how broken my body would be, whether a tree would break my fall or whether I'd simply hit the pavement and be bang, dead, gone. That's when I'd I know if a soul could divorce a body. Would I float back up through the window and then be joyous I was no longer trapped in flesh heaving against gravity? Or would I simply no longer exist? Some days I'm not sure which idea is the more comforting. I turn from the window and face the exercise room.

Exercise beds, walking rails, practice steps, treadmills, and other pieces of equipment are set strategically around the space and, in between, the wounded are corralled. No matter how jubilant the physio staff and orderlies are, the atmosphere seems to settle between grim determination and despondence. It is somewhere twice a day to punctuate the routine in between the meals most of us look forward to, despite sometimes arriving cold or too watery.

Patients here fall into two general categories: the young ones who've been in road accidents and the ageing ones whose bodies are falling apart all by themselves. We're all isolated, sandwiched together, practising some form of denial. The older ones look dazed and disbelieving. The young ones, mostly males, joke with the camaraderie of soldiers, slapping each other on the back, refusing to reveal the pain of crushed and amputated limbs. My genetics put me in the too-hard-basket category and I usually keep to myself. The energy it takes to exercise is enough without trying to make friends. I don't fit in and I don't want to. Most people end up in rehab once or twice in their lives if they're unlucky. I average once or twice every few years. I remind myself I am here to heal.

The orderly wheels me to a twin-sized exercise bed next to an elderly woman who's won the war over getting into day clothes. Her nightie and dressing gown move back and forth as she looks, bleary-eyed, at the hook attached to the metal bars above, the rope coming under her knee in a canvas sling, her heel sliding mechanically in the bandaged donut that moves on a piece of smooth Masonite. I look across, smile and mumble, 'Hi,' just to be polite but there's no response. Her face tells me she doesn't want to be here, or anywhere else. Her mind's off and away. Each time her leg swings out, the smell from her unwashed crotch is powerful. A physio assistant bounces up to me. I look at her, pleading, hoping she'll get the idea I want to go to another bed. I know she can smell what I smell but her smile tightens into a rictus of snap-happiness and I know there's no point in complaining. I look around and see there are no free spaces, anyway.

I sit on the bench under the arms of the peppercorn tree. Some bloke walks stiffly towards me through the self-opening doors and stops, arms crossed, shoulders rigid. The breeze is mild, the sun pale. There is no one else out here. I decide talk is preferable to an awkward silence.

'Looks like you had a hip done,' I say, recognising the gait that looks like something between wearing a heavily padded nappy and coming off a horse after a long ride in the saddle.

'Yeah,' he drawls and flinches. I detect an American twang. He looks to be in a lot of pain.

'You?' he asks.

'Yep, same. Right hip.'

'Me too. Right one. Been a week and a half.' He sucks in through his teeth. Rocks on his heels. I slide across the bench and offer him seat.

'Nope. Rather stand.' He stares off, arms crossed, surveying the horizon.

'I see you're walking without any crutches,' I say. 'Isn't it a bit early to be getting around unaided?'

'Well, that's what the doc ordered but I do things my way. Best way to build up muscle.'

*Best way to dislocate a new hip. If he thinks he's in pain now …* I squint into his face. His broad jaw clenches.

'Mr Tough Guy, hey,' I laugh.

'I guess you could say that. Served in Korea.'

He tells me about getting shot down in a helicopter, dealing with shrapnel wounds, watching his mates being blown up. How am I supposed to respond to this avalanche of bloody reality? All I can say is I have this genetic thing.

'See you 'round,' he says, cranking himself to turn and walk back to his room.

'Yeah, probably time for some painkillers,' I call out.

'Don't believe in 'em,' he calls over his shoulder.

Next day we meet again under the peppercorn tree, me sitting, him standing. He tells me what he does for a living: designs and builds prosthetic eyeballs.

'You ever studied an eyeball?' he asks.

'Well, we had to cut up a sheep's eyeball in biology once,' I say, 'but I was too distressed to look.'

'Well, there's an art to getting the detail right. It's gotta be perfect. Ya gotta match the glass eyeball to the real one to the point where ya can't tell the difference.'

Apparently, there are many different paints and fine brushes to re-create the colour and tracery of eyeballs.

'So, you're an artist,' I say.

'I guess you could say that. No eye just reflects blue or brown. It's like a constellation in there. Matching nature is no mean feat.'

I declare my eyes are hazel and have as many colours as a fruit tingle. We eye each other off. His are black-ringed and flinty grey.

'I heard there's a fish that has eyes split in two,' I say. 'The lower half is designed to see under water and the upper half to see above the water line ...'

'Ya don't say ...'

I recall an eye dream: seated in something like a dentist's chair, a woman and a man are doing something to my face. I don't feel anything but later I discover they have replaced my eyes. They are shinier than the real ones and, on the back, they're covered in artwork, one scene merging spherically into the other. I hold my eye in my hand and admire the fine brushwork. I'm happy. The world is bright, fresh and clear. But then I speak to someone who's had the same procedure and they ask me how I go putting my original eyes back in at night. No one has told me this is something I must do. I can't have my artificial eyes in all the time, she said, otherwise my eyes will become infected and cloud over.

I tell her I have an eye phobia and can't imagine doing this. She says I have no choice. It is best if I learn to do it myself, she says. She tells me about the special pressure point in the soft boneless area around the temples where you squeeze and your eyes pop out. I remember the brown glutinous mess I'd seen splatter on the wall when I was in the chair. The man and the woman had done this squeezing thing swiftly, distracting me with music and chatter. How could I still see even though they had removed my eyes?

Did I know there were a million variations of skin tones? Palette after palette mixed and blended to perfectly match a missing nose, bits of forehead, skulls, jaws, and lips.

Hair follicles were the other challenge.

'Well, aren't we lucky we're only dealing with bits on the inside,' I say, hearing myself sounding a note of brittle cheer. 'Doesn't matter what it looks like in there. My first hip looked like a job done on an old gate, wires and screws every which way. Titanium is lighter and stronger than bone, so I like to see it as an improvement.'

'Well, that's not entirely the case ...'

He shifts his weight about and I can see he's probably stood for long enough but I know there's no point in offering him a seat.

'... bone is heavier if you're doing a direct comparison, by about 1.3 times, but titanium alloy is five times stronger than bone.'

'Well, a twig from this tree is probably stronger than my bones,' I laugh. 'Anyway, I'm off.' I pull myself up on elbow crutches and head towards the door. He turns stiffly and follows.

The late afternoon sun is orange and the gnarly limbs of the peppercorn tree cast me in shadow. I consider going inside just as Mr Hop-along comes out.

'Now, just look to the horizon and tell me what you see,' he says.

'Um, the setting sun, the sky, a fence, couple of trees …'

'No, look harder. Look at what you've missed. What about that bird in the branch. Observation, real observation, vigilance is the key to most every situation …'

*Oh, for fuck's sake!!* I think about bringing a magazine or a book with me next time but such flimsy protection would be futile against this cowboy. He refuses to fit into the walls of this place, as I do. But I make myself small as he makes himself large. I could be rude and ignore him but compliance takes less energy

'Yeah … Tell me how you're getting on. Making progress?'

'Sure. But the doctors aren't happy with me. I even had to fight with them about the operation. I refused to be unconscious while they mucked around with me. Ya lose control, ya lose everything …'

'What!! You were awake when they replaced your hip!? Jesus Christ in a hand basket!'

'Yup. Never been unconscious in my life and I'm not about to start. I agreed to be anaesthetised from the waist down, is all.'

'So, you were awake when they cut you open and used the electric saw to slice off the top of your femur? That's nuts! Once they slice that ball off, blood and marrow spray all over the place. And the hammering they do to get that metal shaft into your bone … you saw all that?'

'Not quite. The compromise was a suspended green sheet so I couldn't see what they were doing. But I heard it all and felt all the wrenching about.'

'Well, if they hadn't put that sheet up, you probably would have got your own blood and marrow as your first meal. Did you pass out at all? The noise alone would've done me in.'

'Course not!' he chuckles, 'Awake through the whole damn thing. If ya wanna know, I was frustrated they put that sheet up. Once I heard that saw go off, I wanted in on the action. Made me curious …'

'I bet you wanted to check those surgeons were following procedure, right?'

'Well, it's my insurance payin' for it.'

'What sort of a control freak are you?'

'The sort that don't get killed.'

'You've got trust issues, mate, that's for sure.'

'You sound like my first wife.'

He goes on to tell me about his second wife and twelve-year-old son. He wants his boy to join the armed forces but the boy's not too keen. Mr Hop-along comes from a long military line so he's not taking no for an answer. I feel sorry for the kid. Then he tells me how often he's compelled to get out the strap.

'The kid needs discipline. How else's he gonna learn? No way I'm bringing up some soft cock faggot.'

'I need some painkillers,' I say, as I struggle to get up. I turn to farewell the peppercorn tree and notice my eyes are shedding tears as if they are not my eyes at all.

# DESCENSUS

*(After the fire a little more had roared—Dante)*

## Into the abyss: besieged and misunderstood

1993. I'm living in several circles of hell with little chance of escape. Across the ocean Bosnia is in a state of war and here, in a rehab hospital in Melbourne, I imagine I'm suffering along with those prisoners in the internment camps. My fellow captives are suffering, too. But I can't help them or myself.

It began with a left hip, worn to bone-on-bone in a false socket halfway up my pelvis. My defective bones needed cutting-edge technology to brace them from their defective, fractured job description. The surgeon said he would have a customised prosthesis made with a lengthened metal rod to be drilled inside my femur. The prototype was to be designed and built in the US. The design drafts were mathematical, architectural, a framework for an internal construction I would never get to see.

> *Which wills, that as the thing more perfect is,*
> *The more it feels of pleasure and of pain*
>
> —DANTE

I sat by the phone waiting for the call that would tell me the construction, fine-tuned to my exact measurements, had arrived and the operation could be booked in. The pain was sharp and grinding, like a rotting tooth in my thigh. I barely left my apartment. Weeks turned into months.

My local GP was reluctant to give me anything too strong for the pain. 'If I give you anything strong, you will soon want something stronger, and we don't know how long you will be waiting for surgery.' He sent me home with an analgesic now banned in several countries due to the risk of heart arrhythmia and death in high doses. The dosage he prescribed barely touched the sides.

> *And what pain is upon you, that so sparkles?*
>
> —DANTE

The call I made to my surgeon's secretary in November 1992 was the broken hope that sent me to Limbo, Dante's first circle of hell. The prosthesis would not be available before Christmas. Jesse, my partner at the time, who worked nightshift as a nurse, found me that afternoon, kneeling on all fours in a bathtub half full of hot water, an animal howl coming from my insides, echoing off the bathroom tiles, a sound I didn't recognise as my own.

I was without thought or reason. Sitting in my local doctor's clinic, I barely knew where I was. The GP listened to my pleas to take the pain way, I wanted the pain to go away, please, please, I needed pethidine, the only thing I knew that could give me relief to help me hold onto whatever kernel of sanity I had left.

I felt this GP might have understood my physical situation more than others because he'd told me his own mother had been diagnosed with hip dysplasia. But I should have realised that, if his mother had given birth to him, her hips were probably not as poorly placed as mine. I sat in his room, barely able to hold my head up. The inflammation from my hip had spread all the way to my shoulder blade. The doctor asked, 'From one to ten, ten being the pain of childbirth, how strong is your pain?'

He damn well knew I didn't have children, had never been pregnant.

It took all my strength not to scream, to keep from falling away from myself. I'd dealt long enough with the medical profession to know that losing it, raising one's voice, did not work in one's favour; I had to play the good girl to get what I wanted, not a troublesome patient to be quietened or dismissed. I was moved to the examination table and given a shot. Almost immediately I went limp, felt suddenly numb. He arranged for me to go to a place for 'respite'.

> *Not causeless is this journey to the abyss*
> —DANTE

The respite place was a private psychiatric hospital. I was so doped up on the powerful relaxant he had injected me with I couldn't think. I was told it was dinnertime and I was to grab myself a tray and help myself to the food laid out bistro-style in the dining room. I stood helpless, trying to hold myself up on elbow crutches with the plastic tray hanging from my fingers. There was no way I could physically get food for myself but apparently it was all about 'independence' and 'personal responsibility' in this house of illness. I was finding it hard to even breathe.

A balding man twice my height came up to me and introduced himself, his grey eyes moving disconcertingly back and forth like a metronome set to allegro. I dropped the tray and fell into the chair closest to me. A staff member came bouncing over with water in a green plastic cup in this glass-forbidden bistro and encouraged me to get food. I had no energy to bother telling her the obvious; I wasn't hungry anyway, I just needed to lie down before I fell down.

I was taken to a twin room. The other bed was empty. I don't remember how I got onto the bed but it wasn't long before I needed to pee. I couldn't remember the last time I'd had a drink but the relaxant meant nothing was holding up or in. I could see the ensuite had no grab rails or any concession towards anyone with mobility issues. I lay there, still feeling the intensity of the pain, though I felt limbless and scared to move without assistance. Before I had the chance to buzz, a young nurse arrived, grinning with such enthusiasm, I wondered if she was possibly another patient. She carried one of those instant polaroid cameras and said, 'Okay, smile, I'm going to take your photo!'

'What for?'

'Oh, just standard procedure. We take photos of all the patients just in case they … get lost or accidentally leave!'

'No! You can't take my photo! I shouldn't even be here. Please, I need pain relief.'

'Well, we'll see about that when the doctor has seen you. Now, I'll just take a quick snap …'

'NO, YOU WON'T!' I screamed.

> *And grief that finds a barrier in the eyes*
> *Turns itself inward to increase the anguish*
> —DANTE

I doubled over and cried into my hands to hide the very thing she was determined to 'snap'. As if I could even get off the bed, let alone escape. The nurse left, with the tight smile of someone who had experienced this sort of disobedience before and knew who would win out in the end.

I was summoned. The psychiatrist wasn't going to come to me, I had to walk down several long corridors to get to his room. I could see the nurse leading me was getting impatient with how slowly I was moving but it was a miracle I could move at all. It took every particle of strength to haul myself forward on a hip that was unusable, a pelvis that was twisted, a spine that was crooked. Apparently not one wheelchair was at hand, probably in the name of 'independence' and 'personal responsibility' except for attempts to escape. I stared at the swirling carpet patterns and kept on until I stopped and said I couldn't go any further. I doubled over, willing myself not to cry. These crazy people were not going to win. The nurse stood and waited. I had no choice but to move the few more metres to the doctor's room where there would be a seat for me.

I sat, spent. The desk was full of papers and behind the papers was the psychiatrist, head down, reading, a gold-tipped quilled pen in his manicured hand. Slim, grey-haired, a tight leather waistcoat, buttoned up over a floral shirt, sleeves neatly rolled, thick gold watch on a tanned forearm.

'Now, tell me why you think you are here …' He over enunciated, still not looking at me.

'I don't know. I'm in terrible pain, I have a dislocated hip, I'm waiting for an operation …'

'Hmmm.'

'And what are you taking for the pain?'

'I don't have any tablets on me and I haven't had any pain relief since I arrived. Please, I need something for the pain.' I leaned over and awkwardly stood up from the chair.

'Please sit down.'

'This chair is too high for me and my back is hurting.'

'Hmmm. I know, you just want to lean over to see what I'm writing …'

'What? No, I'm in PAIN! I can't stay in one position for long. And I had to walk so far …'

'Hmmm. Well, I'm putting you on valium and (something-or-other-else that wasn't for pain), and I'll book you tomorrow for group therapy.'

'What?? What do you mean?'

'This is clearly far more than organic.'

'I don't need therapy, I need pain relief,' I bleated feebly. My faint, but still fluttering senses, knew that to make a scene would swallow me further into the belly of the psych beast.

'You can go now.'

'It's too far for me to walk back to my room.'

'I'll call for a nurse.'

I was led to a small meeting room not far from the psychiatrist's office. Numb and defeated, I fell into a slightly more comfortable chair. The door was closed on me. I was free to cry. The door flew open midstream and a nurse and another staff member entered. Word had gone out and family had arrived. The staff were calm and oh so reasonable as they explained the recommendation that I stay, based on the psychiatrist's consultation. I don't remember the conversation, just Mum looking at me clearly asking, 'Do you want to stay or do you want to go home?'

'Home!'

'Right, let's go then.'

It was only when in the carpark Mum confirmed my worst suspicions: if I'd stayed overnight, I would have been involuntarily committed. I was bundled back to the apartment exhausted and with still no pain relief.

> *Even as the flowerets, by nocturnal chill,*
> *Bowed down and closed, when the sun whitens them,*
> *Uplift themselves all open on their stems;*
> *Such I became with my exhausted strength*
>
> —DANTE

By mid-afternoon the next day something snapped. Why hadn't I thought of going to emergency? To the hospital where my surgery was planned? That GP completely deceived me and my partner by stating that he was sending me for respite when what he was doing was putting me in a private psychiatric hospital! The emergency doctor on duty took one look at the inflamed hip, and the swelling that had reached to my shoulder blade.

'Oh, you poor thing.'

Ten blessed minutes later I was breathing the lifeblood of pethidine, tingling beyond skin or thought or gravity. That, and a script for the strongest combination of paracetamol and codeine available—just enough to pause the pain loop, and recalibrate until—when, when, when?

The custom-designed prosthesis finally arrived. I was knocked into unconsciousness and cut open. The surgeon sawed off the ball of my femur and began drilling down to make room for the metal rod. He stopped abruptly, the drill paused millimetres from what had grown into solid bone. At the point of every healed fracture, of which I'd had many, more bone is produced but no one could have predicted or seen that the bone had grown into the marrow cavity without opening me up. Had the drill continued, the largest bone in my body would have shattered. The prosthesis, eight months in the making, was disposed of and an off-the-rack hip replacement used.

I was in the acute ward for two weeks, receiving regular pethidine injections for post-operative pain. My leg was covered with a pressure stocking to prevent blood clots. The rehab hospital was next door but run by a separate institution. On the day of the transfer, I was officially discharged from acute care at around 9.30 a.m. Around 11 a.m. a nursing attendant arrived with a manual wheelchair. It was getting to that time when I needed pain relief, especially as I was being moved, but I was told I'd have to wait until I was admitted and seen by the rehab doctor before I could receive medication of any kind. The nurse took me to rehab via a direct walkway, which was covered in loose gravel. Wheelchairs are not designed for loose gravel. I felt every bump and wobble. By the time we entered a side door even my jaw was aching. My hip had become a growing agony. The smooth lino was a relief of sorts, though I was beyond feeling anything other than the pain overriding almost every other thought or sensation. I was rolled and transferred into a four-bed ward. I asked when the doctor would arrive. I needed pain relief, a pethidine injection; I was allergic to morphine in any other form. No doctor would see me, I was told, until at least 2 p.m., which was admission time.

The coordination between the two hospitals regarding patient transition seemed non-existent. I didn't know how I was going to survive another three hours. The phone on the bedside table was my only hope. I rang until I got a family member. They arrived with a tab of paracetamol and codeine. I surreptitiously dry-swallowed two tablets. I cried until the edge was taken off about forty minutes later. I remember holding someone's hand, maybe one of my sisters, maybe Mum's? The wait was the wait of forever.

Rehab hell begins in earnest with a nurse and an admission form. She pulls up a chair and asks me questions I shouldn't have to answer right now. Her clipped, Chinese accent is difficult for me to understand. All I can think of is 2 p.m.

What is your name?
Date of birth?
What operation did you have?
What was the date of operation?

> *Midway upon the journey of our life I found myself*
> *within a forest dark,*
> *For the straightforward pathway had been lost*
>
> —DANTE

By the time a doctor sees me I am so depleted the pethidine injection hardly registers. My pain tolerance, so high most of the time, has abandoned me. My central nervous system has been flayed raw. It is coiling, vulnerable. I am without skin, my innards slipping from their moorings.

A week into rehab and I haven't left the bed and neither have my three other roommates. Our room is the never-ending waiting room of Limbo but the other circles of hell are hovering, visible only to those of us who lie broken. Whatever sins we may have brought with us are not relevant here. We are as innocent as those unbaptised babies committed to Purgatory. The young woman next to me, a ballet dancer, has her right leg in traction, hanging in a half-bent position. It has been crushed in a car accident. As she pulls herself up by her arms to relieve the pressure of lying in one position the traction squeaks in protest. The woman diagonally opposite has also been in a car accident. She has a crushed pelvis, among other things, and is forced to lie on her back until the pieces of her, pinned internally, become stable. If she tries to sit, even a little, she is overwhelmed with nausea. They both assume I have also been in an accident.

'I was born an accident,' I sigh, wrecking their assumptions of me being a sudden victim of happenstance. The woman opposite me is quiet. She is old and perhaps barely clinging on.

I am now under the care of the doctor in charge of rehab, though my surgeon comes to check in on me after the first week. He says I've been on pethidine for three weeks and that is enough. I need to start on oral pain relief, which means paracetamol and codeine. The rehab doctor, on the other hand, decides I needed to continue the injections a little longer. He has seen enough of me to know I am far from coping with anything less at this stage.

*My course is set for an uncharted sea*

—DANTE

The 1990s still held the fear of patient opioid addiction because of the incorrect belief that administered appropriately or not, even short-term use, let alone mid- to long-term use would inevitably lead to psychological addiction. Clinical findings in the field of pain today confirm that the phenomenon of abuse is observed very rarely. While opioid abuse has increased in western countries, particularly in the US, if the pain-relief delivered matches the pain relief required, psychological addiction almost never occurs—especially if the patient doesn't have the risk factors for addiction. There are a raft of risk factors, including genetics and environment, but I, for one, appear to have little to no risk factors except that I periodically require strong pain relief, especially pre- and post-operatively. It comes with the territory.

My surgeon had no idea of what I'd been through to this point. He only ever saw me, briefly, when I was conscious. The longest time a surgeon ever spends with a patient is when they are under the knife. My usual ability to cope with pain had been reduced to zero. As my pain had continued to increase, my tolerance decreased and my pain receptors went from blocking to releasing the agony like a burst dam. Now the medical profession understands that keeping on top of pain by administering pain relief before things became unbearable is the best way to manage pain. I instinctively knew that this was true. My instincts also told me not take a certain dose for too long because then one ended up needing more and more for the same amount of relief. I would periodically cut down my dose of paracetamol and codeine combinations and endure stronger pain until a lower dose worked. Fortunately, I do not have an addictive personality and had never, and would never be, psychologically addicted to pain-killers, alcohol or anything else. Despite my condition, optimum health is something I aim for. Otherwise I'd have become an alcoholic or drug addict and would probably be six feet under by now. Instead, I have become my own expert pain specialist.

There are now two separate drug charts to choose from— the surgeon's recommendations and the rehab specialist's. This is the crack through which several circles of Dante's hell compete to torment me: the fifth, eighth and ninth circles of Anger, Fraud and Treachery.

*I did not die, and I alive remained not*

—DANTE

The atmosphere in my rehab ward does not promote healing. It is about frustrated and overworked nurses who are paid less than their acute hospital counterparts, and who are sick and tired of dealing with the likes of us. I ask for a bedpan and am given no toilet paper. I ask for toilet paper and have a whole roll plonked on my bedside tray covered in spilled water. I am rough handled when I'm given a bed wash, my tight pressure stocking is yanked so fiercely I cry out. The nurse throws her hands up in the air and stomps off.

My physical pain is contained only when, after requesting pain relief, a nurse returns with a pethidine injection. It means the nurse has stumbled upon the rehab's and not the surgeon's drug chart. It is pure luck, a wheel that begins spinning once I buzz for the nurse and stops around twenty minutes later when the nurse on duty returns. If the nurse returns with a little plastic cup with two pills, I know I'm in for an agonising four hours. My only hope of another 'needle' is when the next shift comes on. I end up calling pethidine a 'needle' when I realise that even knowing the name of a drug labels me a possible addict. I learn to keep quiet, to not beg, to wait for the outcome of this mad Russian roulette I am at the mercy of. After a few days I cannot stop the whimpering animal noises that keep escaping from my throat but seem to come from elsewhere. I start seeing myself floating on the ceiling, anything at all to try to escape the inescapable. The system is all wrong and no one seems to care.

*Of those things only should one be afraid*
*Which have the power of doing others harm;*
*Of the rest, no: because they are not fearful*

—DANTE

Nights are the worst. My room isn't far from the nurses' station and those on night duty chatter and laugh raucously without any consideration for those of us lying helpless in our beds of unrelenting rest. I only ever sleep a few hours at a time and only when I get a 'needle'. Every night nurse seems to resent having to answer a call button, but there is one so treacherously cruel, her enjoyment of another's suffering is obvious. Only a night nurse can get away with the behaviour she dishes out. Even when I don't press my bell for assistance she stands in the doorway and stares me down with her cruel, half-smiling mouth. 'Who the fuck do you think you are? You aren't the only one in this hospital. Now shut your face so these other patients can sleep and we can all get some peace.'

She watches calmly, with sadistic enjoyment, when one night I have to stuff tissues into my mouth to quash the noises I have no control over. If I ever sleep, it is out of sheer exhaustion and then I wake myself up with my own groaning. I dream I am not in a rehab hospital in Melbourne but in Bosnia. I am behind wire, I am being starved, ethnically cleansed. I cry out to my captors.

The woman with the fractured pelvis starts to complain about me. I make surreptitious phone calls to friends and family with the handset under the bedcovers, begging someone to help. I am probably not making any sense. No one seems to believe what's going on.

The rehab doctor comes to see me but, by this time, I can hardly string a sentence together. I feel my core slipping away. The doctor says he will check and fix the problem of the two 'alleged' drug charts.

Nothing changes. I begin to hallucinate. I am beyond my body, floating, seeing faces of people I have never known. The light disappears. I am far away, yet cocooned in cotton sheets, foetal, unmoving. Two nurses come to my bed and unlock its wheels. They are taking me away. Suddenly I am in another room all by myself. A single room, with a view too bright. I pull my arm over my eyes and lie as still as still is still. Everything falls away until I feel weight on the mattress. It is the rehab doctor with his young son. It is Saturday, apparently. He tells me I have been moved to another ward. I turn my head just enough to see his face. He looks pale. I tell him about the night nurse and the tissues in my mouth. I hear myself speaking in a slow monotone. He says nothing but his eyes redden and tears fall. His young son holds his hand silently, looking a little confused.

## A fundamental shift: in conversation with a wound-licking body-soul

Once I felt safe my healing began and the chemistry in my brain shifted. There was no professional commentary, no formal diagnoses. I was my own observational tool, both patient and physician in conversation with a wound-licking body-soul. I was wheeled to hydrotherapy and made friends in the pool. I took to crutch-walking my way across a busy road from rehab to the nearest pub where I got to know the publican, a retired AFL player, and his wife who served beers in between pouring vodka shots for herself. My natural tendency to observe before committing to conversation fell away. I talked to anyone who came through the door, laughed and joked and hatched a plan.

Back in my rehab bed, I lay awake most nights writing stories and songs and poetry. I felt one with every worldly imagining, every living thing, every television image. My mind didn't just take in the universe, it *was* the universe. If I looked into the distance I saw the faces of people I'd never met passing as if flashing on an invisible screen. I was in thrall to sensations and images and ideas coming so fast they spilled round me like confetti. How to hold onto it all? I laughed with an urgency and carelessness because nothing and everything mattered. Time raced so fast its motion was barely perceptible. Night and day merged. Then I was discharged.

At home, Jesse and I continued at a pace that delighted me. Jesse had been through so much with me that he was a little thrown by this sudden rush of positive creativity. It felt like I was on fire, making up for all the weeks, months, years I'd been left out, incapacitated with something-or-other. In a matter of weeks, I pulled together a 'Hip Party' performance with music and stand-up. I called in my brother and a couple of friends to form a band, negotiated a gig at the pub across the road from the hospital, and invited everyone I knew, including hospital staff.

The pub was packed as I grabbed the microphone and sang, 'I'm a hip young chick with bad old bones ...' It was a great night, a little crazy but I didn't care. I was thirty-two years old and back in the game. Or so I thought.

I decided to go it alone. It was wrenchingly difficult but things hadn't been good between me and Jesse for a long time. We'd fallen into an unhealthy co-dependence of caregiver and care-recipient. He was a very good carer, especially being employed as a nurse, but I knew that looking after me had come at the expense of his own wants and needs. At that stage I assumed I was bisexual: being with a man felt more socially acceptable and had certainly been more acceptable as far as my family went and the last thing I needed was more drama in my life. But I knew staying wasn't fair to either of us and I also knew by then that I really wanted to be with a woman. As much as Jesse was gentle, kind and artistic and we could talk for hours about so many things, it was time for me to let go of the safety net. I'd had a couple of relationships with women before I met Jesse, which I'd been completely open about and I needed to return to that world.

I moved from our art deco apartment in Elsternwick to a friend-of-a-friend's room in Port Melbourne. It was a rundown worker's cottage in a narrow street with few trees or space for front gardens. My room was a box with a tiny window looking out onto a rear concrete path, sunlight never quite reaching the grubby white walls. As much as leaving the relationship was the right thing to do, I felt a rising anxiety. I'd been through so much and I was suddenly confronted with the realisation that I was still incredibly emotionally fragile. What had I done? I wanted this to be a new beginning but felt like I was constantly teetering on the edge of an indefinable dread.

The first indication of how this domestic arrangement with my new housemate would work out occurred in the kitchen. There wasn't a lot of storage space so she had put some shelves on the wall. I placed my precious pieces of red and gold crockery on the shelf and went about setting up my bedroom. A few minutes later a great crashing sound startled me and I went back to the kitchen. There, strewn across the beige lino, was my red and gold crockery reduced to a pile of shards. I stood, tears pricking, as my housemate bustled up the hall from her front room. Chunks had come out of the wall and the shelf lay on the floor, its particle board innards sprinkled over the whole mess like a crusty garnish. My housemate glared. 'What happened?'

'I think you can see what happened,' I said, trying not to show how much this felt like a symbolic shattering of my life. No glue was going to put this Humpty Dumpty mess back together.

'You put too much on there!' she said.

There was no point in saying anything. From what I could see, it looked like the shelf would have collapsed no matter what was put on it. It hadn't been screwed or nailed into anything but plaster. We swept it all away into the bin and pretended nothing had happened but the disaster made for a cool stand-off.

I returned to my job as an Industry Training Consultant at the Council of Adult Education in the city. I worked with companies to create effective training plans for their shop-floor staff and provided communication training for management. It was at the height of compulsory competitive tendering and restructures and all the myriad upheavals Victoria was experiencing under Jeff Kennett's Premiership. My CAE colleagues were the best bunch of old left-wing ratbags you could find. We rejoiced and moaned together against the powers that wanted to see the likes of us gone. We believed in education for its own sake and couldn't or wouldn't understand that to grade our 'students' according to assessment and outcomes systems made no sense in our line of work. We railed against ordinary people becoming nameless 'units'. We wrestled with the political correctness that had us arguing over whether it was sexist to call an educational toolkit a toolkit and should we call it an educational sewing kit for a bit of balance? Old frameworks were standing on shaky stumps.

I loved that my office looked over Degraves Street, a busy pedestrian lane opposite Flinders Street Station, full of quirky shops and trendy eateries. Lunchtimes were always an adventure. But I was finding it more and more difficult to get myself going every morning. At work it became harder to concentrate. I thought it was just symptoms of Chronic Fatigue Syndrome I'd developed over the last few years, but I soon realised it was more than that. I stared out of my office window at the pigeons who regularly landed to heckle and fornicate, their droppings a thick layer on the sill. I sometimes lost track of time, caught up in some sort of non-thinking trance. Then I'd shake myself off and grab a coffee.

## Other lands—two: an island getaway

1994. It was a winter break from my job at the Council of Adult Education. I walked with a stick because there was continuous pain in my left leg, but I'd become so accustomed to it I kept blocking it out. I just remember limping into a travel agent not far from work and asking them to send me somewhere warm.

Anywhere I could rest and loosen the cold from my bones. They sent me to Fiji.

Every night at the resort a band of guitars serenaded us while we were encouraged to drink kava, the local muddy drink that had an effect similar to smoking weed. The sun and the kava melted me into one of the banana lounges beside the chlorinated pool, where I spent most of my time reading and sipping cocktails. It seemed I was the only single tourist in this gated resort. Young couples smooched half naked and older couples quietly worked through the all-you-can-eat menu. I'm not sure where I felt more alone: here or Port Melbourne.

I struggled to walk through the imported sand with my walking stick. I would have liked to bob in the ocean, but it was crammed with stingers. My palm-fronded hut was only a few metres from shore and at night the waves broke in an unrelenting rush that kept me awake most of the night. It took days before I found it soothing.

I hired a car and drove away from the 'compound' resting on imported sand fringed with ocean nasties. The locals lived on straggly blocks with dwellings thrown together in a mix of concrete bricks and corrugated iron. One man told me the resort I was staying at had taken the area's best fishing spot.

I drove to Suva, the capital, which danced with the colourful sarongs of the large Indian-Fijian population. Descended from Indian indentured labourers shipped to work in the local sugarcane fields, modern Indian-Fijians dominated Fiji's business world. Native Fijians were the disenfranchised ones. I returned to my gated resort of stolen sand and waters where everyone smiled.

## Losing the plot

Back in Port Melbourne, as the months wore on, I saw less colour. Everything seemed a version of grey or charcoal. Then it turned black. The road, the sky, people, my bedroom. I only noticed light when it was so bright I cowered from it. My head hurt and a heaviness gathered round my guts. I felt as if I was being pushed into the ground into a dark, grainy existence. Someone taught me how to do yogic breathing and I lay on my Jenny Kee crazily colourful doona cover trying to turn my chest and belly into a rhythmic figure eight of deep breaths. I closed my eyes but when I opened them they landed on the grubby white ceiling with the pearly grey light bulb dangling over my head like a cataract.

I felt more shattered than my shattered crockery. I started to wonder what it would be like to drive into a pole or off a pier to make the black permanent. I was so tired my whole body felt like concrete wading through treacle. Was this how Virginia Woolf felt when she took her final walk to the river, pockets filled with the weight of the world?

I caught myself in reflections and hardly recognised myself. I avoided the bathroom mirror, putting my makeup on through half-lidded eyes. I was thin, pale, empty. My appetite for anything had become a vague memory.

I went to a psychologist. He told me I had slipped behind the veil to a colourless world that, if I continued, would descend to the pit of the black dog where, at its base, the will to die could override every other emotion. The psychologist said I talked about my emotions and the bad things that had happened to me without actually feeling those emotions. He told me I had to find a way to stop intellectualising my feelings. He suggested writing a diary. I bought a notebook and started writing my feelings but this only made me feel worse. A full stop felt like a death sentence. I couldn't even cry.

At home I lay on the sofa and felt something move beneath my skin. It had been over a year since my left hip replacement. The scar on my left thigh had completely healed but beneath the scar tissue, something was shifting. I pressed the area and it depressed then sprang back out again. I did this a few more times, fascinated and horrified at this strange mechanism playing out below my muscle.

An X-ray showed a small plate with loosened screws and the fracture that was forcing the plate away from the bone. I had been getting around with a fractured leg for a year, gradually absorbing the pain as the whole thing was falling apart. I was so used to dealing with physical pain my brain had found a way of blocking it out and morphing it into mental pain, compounding the inevitable depression I experienced following my manic episode a year before. I was diagnosed with secondary depression, not because of a mood disorder so much as a natural reaction to the extreme physical states of my body.

As had happened a few years before with my right femur, where it had fractured from the prosthetic shaft being hammered into my too-thin bones, I was wheeled into surgery and had everything braced. Once healed, my brain chemistry returned to a healthier equilibrium. The bipolar extremes slipped away and I welcomed the light and colours of the world again.

# THE MUSCULARITY
# OF THE HEART

**Finding my humans: pulse points of love**

I was ten years old the first time I was told I was 'sexy'. One of the school teachers had devised a musical performance following a trip to the Philippines. She had us all darken our skin in a bath of Condy's Crystals and dress in Philippine fluffy blouses and long skirts and we did a traditional dance amongst two long wooden sticks being clapped rhythmically on the ground. I must have looked quite exotic with my brown curls and hazel eyes and my skin awash with fake melanin. The teacher had made the whole process sound so exciting we were all sucked in. She'd left on a jet plane, travelled across the ocean and returned with a bag of cultural accoutrements from a place we'd never heard of where dark-skinned people danced in the streets and were perpetually happy. And, she told me, her face broad with enthusiasm, that I looked 'sexy'.

'What does that mean, sexy?' I asked, with all the innocence of a sheltered kid at a Catholic primary school run by nuns in the early 1970s. (I heard years later one nun was so sheltered herself that she had to ask what 'fart' meant!)

The teacher smiled at my confusion and her eyes laughed, 'Well, it means you look very ... lovely.'

On the night of the school performance, I awkwardly hopscotched barefooted in and around the moving sticks trying to avoid being clapped on the ankles as they came together. I'd already collected a few bruises in rehearsals but of course the Condy's Crystals disguised the marks despite it slipping from my skin onto my puffy blouse like brown skid marks. I wonder if any of the adults considered the possibility that clapping sticks could have given me fractures. Luckily that didn't happen, but my hips hurt with the movement. I couldn't let the audience down though, and especially the teacher who I now also considered sexy. I soldiered on and probably would have hopscotched amongst those sticks all night if she'd asked me to.

I never hung out with groups in primary school or high school. I usually gravitated to single female friendships that were intense and inevitably burned themselves out. At high school, when each of my girlfriends began talking non-stop about boys and then turned up at school wearing turtle necks or scarves to hide their 'love bites' I knew I wasn't like them. Back then Frankston was the 'end of the line'—a place where bogans ran feral and where the heavy iron gates of Stella Maris Ladies' College failed to keep the tawdry or the hormones at bay. If the girls weren't pashing boys and smoking in the bushes lining the school's perimeter, they were skiving off to the beach starring in their own version of *Puberty Blues* with their surfer boyfriends. Others were proud of their status as supermarket checkout chicks or milk-bar girls. These were never employment possibilities for me with my limited standing and walking abilities. Those girls had boys and money to burn while I was the nerdy kid doing well at school, taking piano lessons and getting fifty cents a week pocket money from Dad.

All that changed when I met my first boyfriend, Brendan. I was sixteen. He was two years older and had a status beyond anything I could hope for—his own car and a full-time job as a mechanic.

I was flattered that he was interested in me and he turned out to be a good kisser. His Dad was a fireman and our first big date was going to the local fireman's ball. I wore something far too dressy for the occasion and got scared when, after the ball, Brendan decided to scream his car up Oliver's Hill, Frankston's most romantic hangout where most nights the car park was chockers with panel vans and steaming windows. Brendan had a large sedan, but this was the age of those vans we called fuck trucks. Open the back door of one of those babies and you'd see a double mattress and walls lined with shag pile. Everyone used to joke, 'if the van's a rockin' don't come a knockin'. Brendan laughed at my screams of terror as he sped around doing wheelies on the gravel. I was afraid of two things that night—I didn't want to imagine how my bones would fare in a collision and I was terrified of becoming pregnant. I was never going to fit in with the mob on Oliver's Hill.

I knew I wasn't going out with Brendan for the right reasons and it didn't take long before he ended up giving me the talk that I wasn't THE ONE. Even at nineteen he was searching for his future wife and both of us guessed I probably wasn't wife material. A few boyfriends later I still hadn't felt the pull of wifedom or baby making. I began to wonder whether I was the problem.

Then there was Rachel, blonde-haired, blue-eyed, and a little taller than me. It was a trip to Tasmania in 1979, and in that long stretch of summer between school and adulthood we found ourselves locked out of a youth hostel after missing the 10 p.m. curfew. Breaking the rules felt like freedom but the reality wasn't so exciting. Should we sleep in the nearby sand dunes? No! We could be raped and murdered. Could we just lie here and sleep on the grass? Maybe, but it looked like rain …

'Hey, shut up and take this tent, will ya! We're trying to sleep.' The voices came from some disembodied hostellers shovelling a tent bag through the rear ground floor window. We thanked them in a loud whisper and tried putting the tent up in the dark without making a ruckus. Of course, we dissolved into stifled giggles a few times until we got it sorted but there were no further noise complaints.

Our first kiss was in that tent set up in the hostel's backyard. It felt thrilling, dangerous and instinctive. From there we spent the rest of the time on the Apple Isle holding hands imagining ourselves as vagabonds, sucking on tubes of condensed milk by the roadside when we ran out of food. At Port Arthur, we wandered through the crumbling evidence of one of the worst penal colonies in Australia and felt the weight of our sexual transgression. From the first settlement to the time we were travelling, male homosexuals had been criminalised and lesbians were meant to be invisible. However, we regained courage when visiting the remnants of the Cascades Female Factory just south of Hobart. The factory, set up to foster 'proper feminine behaviour' in women convicts felt equally haunted but, as the *Colonial Times* reported in 1841, the place had apparently been a 'hotbed of lesbian vice' dominated by the so-called lesbian 'flash mob' named for their flash clothing that included repurposing prison attire into masculine-style garb. It all felt wonderfully rebellious despite the horrendous conditions in which the women worked.

Our own personal rebellion occurred during the overnight trip back across Bass Strait when we abandoned our uncomfortable economy seats on the ship for a small storage room filled with baby cots and brooms. In the stuffy darkness we drifted in and out of sleep cosied up under our coats on the hard floor, buffeted by rocking waves, scared we could be exposed as stowaways as we practiced the 'unholy sisterhood' of our convict forebears. Back on the mainland we declared our love for each other. Six months later it was over. Still, the experience took me closer to finding my humans.

Georgia, my next girlfriend, was purposefully butch, angry and bereaved. She was a couple of years older than me. Pale, with mousy hair and the eyes of a child despite her brave exterior, I fell for her vulnerability. Georgia had just lost her mother to cancer and was holed up in an Edwardian mansion on a hill in Melbourne's inner north. An older lesbian couple had recently purchased the place, which was rundown and still housed a couple of residents from when it had been a men's boarding house. They were very kind to the elderly men who had nowhere else to go. The large kitchen, where they prepared food for everyone, was filled with the pungent odour of overripe fruit and vegetables and buzzing with flies. I sensed the two women were out of their depth. The renovation attempts seemed half-hearted. They'd probably bought it for a song and had little money to do the place up. (Today it has had the full overhaul by someone with means and is worth millions.)

Georgia was living in a run-down bedroom on the top floor. The owners were the sort of lesbians that took all women, and particularly lesbians, into their fold. They had probably bought the place with the idea of setting up some ideal lesbian commune. Apart from the sad old men living around its edges, the house was lesbian-centric with photos and paintings of women such as Virginia Woolf and Vita Sackville-West hanging on the walls. The two gave Georgia the warmth of unconditional lesbian mother love, which is exactly what she needed. I had entered another world and saw that a life, different from my upbringing, was truly possible. However, I was a little taken aback when the two women entered Georgia's room early one morning and chatted comfortably on the end of the bed as we lay together naked under the sheets. Everything that had been taboo while I was growing up suddenly became normal. It was difficult to process.

Georgia and I lasted longer than Rachel and I but in the end she made me feel like I didn't belong. She was militant and judgemental and couldn't handle that sometimes I wore skirts or dresses. Her butch friends admonished me for not particularly liking the lesbian folk music of Judy Small. I wasn't working class enough. I wasn't political enough. I was too 'intellectual'. I was told I couldn't possibly be a true lesbian. Georgia left the house on the hill and I returned to the safety of a more conventional, albeit alternative, existence.

After Georgia I got together with Jesse, my only serious long-term boyfriend who supported me through a series of hellish medical disasters. He was a gentle, artistic type and I admired his paintings and his street cred. He wasn't like other men I'd met. He could have been gay, but he was straight. He'd been to art school with the likes of Nick Cave and hung out with some pretty cool people. I started going out to nightclubs like the Stardust Ballroom in St Kilda and Inflation in the city. I soaked up the punk-cum-new-romantic vibe, wearing lots of black, dayglo socks and Doc Martens. I dyed and teased my hair, wore purple lipstick and drew artistic squiggles on my face with black eyeliner. I pranced around in velvet and lace and soaked up Jesse's impressive record collection. I took Jesse home to meet my mother. She was relieved I at last had a boyfriend but was uncomfortable because we'd moved in together and were living in sin.

Jesse and I bonded over discussions of films and books and music while listening to Dead Can Dance, Joy Division and The Smiths on the turntable. Nihilism was de rigueur. We began sculpting our hair into severe shapes and collecting kitsch from out-of-the-way op shops along with art deco lamps and smoking tables. Everything was deemed ironic. It was the 80s after all. We were carried along with the arrogance of youth. Many people saw us as the ideal couple. I even told Jesse I was attracted to women too and we joked that it was just another thing we had in common. When my body failed me, he cared for me in every way imaginable. It was safe but it felt too safe. We had become more like brother and sister or close friends rather than lovers. As one mutual friend observed, I wanted to be in the sun and he wanted to live under a rock. I wasn't clear about my sexuality. I wasn't being true to the sisterhood. Eventually I understood I wasn't being true to myself.

One of the most difficult things I had to face was coming out to mutual friends after I decided I had to move on from Jesse though I know I broke his heart. I was in my early thirties and needed time to sort myself out.

Along the way there were other lovers before and after those mentioned here. Then I met THE ONE.

## Julienne and the season of sunflowers—one

1995. Julienne was electric. Wild. She bounced into the backyard Christmas party wearing jodhpurs, swanky RM Williams boots and a linen shirt. Her hair was an unruly mop. As I set up my keyboard ready to accompany the ritual carol singing, Julienne came over and introduced herself with a firm handshake and an offer of a drink. Throughout the carols Julienne kept me supplied with alcohol and nibbles and began drumming rhythmically on every surface, sometimes sitting beside me and singing out of key, as I tried to keep playing. Later I learned she had been a drummer in an all-women band and couldn't sing to save herself.

Unsurprisingly I had too much to drink that night and slept in a caravan in the host's backyard. It was only in the bleary-eyed morning I discovered she had spent the night with the host, with whom she was in a relationship of sorts. Strange that I hadn't noticed anything between them during the party.

After breakfast, as I was about to leave, Julienne grabbed me before I reached the front door and, with no one else in view, surreptitiously planted a kiss on my lips. I was captivated.

Sleep deprived and feeling like I'd undergone some sort of cellular transformation, I paced the carpet in my flat and wondered when I would see her again. Julienne had told me she lived in a central Victorian town called Maldon and worked at the Bendigo Library. I could have contacted the library, but it was a Sunday and she was still in Melbourne. I rang the party house and willed her to be the one to answer the phone. Of course, it was the host who answered and before I could think I made up some story about some lost earrings I might have left in the caravan out the back. She put the phone down and went to look and again I willed Julienne to pick up. After a few agonising seconds she did.

'So, how's the little black critter?' she asked, referring to the black outfit I'd worn the night before.

I don't recall what I said but a couple of hours later she was on my doorstep, a grinning Cheshire Cat wearing wraparound sunglasses.

Three weeks later she said, 'I think I should marry you.'

'I think you should too,' I said not missing a beat. What was I saying? How much did I even know about this woman? If a man had said this to me three weeks into dating, I would have spotted several red flags and fled. How many times had I heard of such whirlwind romances ending in tears or worse? What made me so sure that she was THE ONE? I didn't even believe there was such a thing.

And there *were* red flags:

She was already in a relationship, however casual. In fact she admitted to having several lovers at the time.

She was thirteen years older than me.

She drank and smoked too much.

All I can say is there was something beyond the giddy feeling of chemical attraction. It was a knowing deep in my breaky bones.

It was the season of sunflowers. She showered me with them, their sunny faces, bunches and bunches of them. All the possible red flags fell away with each yellow petal, as did her other lovers.

Six months earlier Julienne had purchased an 1850s miner's cottage in Maldon and she was in the middle of renovations.

The move to Maldon had been a knee-jerk reaction to the grief of her father's death closely followed by a nasty break-up. She suddenly abandoned the mud-brick house in Heathcote she'd lovingly built over twelve years and escaped by purchasing a dilapidated dwelling many would have thought best razed to the ground. As she began to work on securing its foundations, Julienne's own foundations crumbled.

Julienne saw herself as tough, can-do, no bullshit. She believed mental illness was a weakness, something that captured only those who lacked willpower. The shock of losing control floored her completely.

'It was as if my soul had left my body,' she said.

She not only felt an absence of soul, it was as if the ground could no longer hold her up and a constant sensation of impending doom lodged itself where she imagined her soul had been. She hadn't slept well for months and found herself shaking uncontrollably. She told me stories of friends rescuing her out of gutters after drinking herself into oblivion. She became terrified of sleeping alone in the dark. The company of multiple lovers and passing out drunk helped her block the terror. She could barely eat.

This was a lot to take in. I wasn't so naive as to think I could put a band-aid over it all but something important was happening between us.

Julienne showed me a recent documentary for which she had been interviewed as the manager of Bendigo's mobile library service. An ABC-TV crew had accompanied her to all the surrounding towns and schools as she drove her prime mover carrying at least five thousand books in the rear. Julienne loved her job and I could see she enchanted all who stepped through the portal of her library on wheels. She chatted to everyone as if they were best of friends. Her love of community and her love of books were palpable.

A couple of months after I met Julienne she asked me to move in with her.

'I was never sure why I bought this little old cottage. Now I know it was because you were about to come into my life,' she said.

I'd never lived in the country before. And I'd not long settled into living in my little rented flat in St Kilda where the local shopping strip was Acland Street with its famous European cake shops and the beach a few minutes away. I was living the fashionable, edgy, alternative life I'd always envisaged. And I'd never lived more than a bike ride's away from a shoreline, a salty breeze on my skin. Maldon would be a complete contrast— a quaint little historic town that was hot, dry and landlocked, and scarred with last century's gold-rush diggings. I told her I'd have to think about it.

A week later a notice arrived from my landlord stating the whole block was up for sale and I had four weeks to move out. I took this as a sign to move in with Julienne even though it meant leaving everything, including my well-paid job teaching academic English skills to overseas students. However, the scariest thing would be telling Mum why I was suddenly moving to central Victoria when I'd never expressed a desire to live anywhere except inner city Melbourne.

I asked Mum to meet me at a cafe in the city. It somehow felt safer being in neutral territory. When I told her I was in love with a woman she blanched. It was bad enough when she'd found out about my previous relationship with Rachel prior to my twenty-first birthday party. That discovery, with many tears and tissues around the dining room table, came close to having my at-home celebration being cancelled with Mum throwing up her hands declaring, 'What will we do with the cake?'

Once Jesse had come along, despite her disapproval of us living together out of wedlock, she put Rachel down to being just a phase. The realisation that her thirty-something daughter was moving away to live with a woman hit her with such force that she said, 'You're still my daughter and I'll always love you and be there for you, but I don't want you to mention her name ever again.'

Every time I rang Mum, I worked hard to keep Julienne out of the conversation. It took a year before she relented and, despite her not approving of my 'lifestyle', Mum reluctantly admitted she had never seen me happier.

Julienne and I exchanged rings and personal vows in February 1996 beneath tall eucalyptus, ancient rocks and a view across the harbour to the Sydney Opera House. Same-sex marriage was years away but we did it anyway with nature and a bottle of champagne as witness. Photos of us on that day show us suntanned and glowing. I was so ecstatic I jumped fully clothed into the sea.

We were crazy-happy. Of course, it wasn't always champagne and sunflowers but we understood each other to the point where we often finished each other's sentences. We held fancy-dress dinner parties. We sat around bonfires drumming on djembes watching fire twirlers under a clear ocean of stars. We hung out with people who'd built their own mud-brick houses with tree-trunk floors and sod roofs. We splash-danced over puddles in our gumboots. We climbed Mount Tarrengower and breathed in the dry, pungent air as we spied on the comings and goings of our little town.

Once, on a visit to Daylesford, Julienne took out her wallet to pay for something and a couple of cicada wings fell to the floor. 'Have you seen my faery wings?' she asked as if it was the most natural thing to say. I cocked my head quizzically like a puppy and she smiled. This was how she related to children. They followed her around as if she were the Pied Piper, often to the bottom of her garden where she would whisper into little shell ears that this was where the faeries lived. I almost believed that she believed.

It aligned with her view of the world that in the most ordinary of things there was magic.

We planned to travel to Europe in 2000 but then the opportunity to go to the United States with Tony Backhouse's gospel tour came up in late 1999 and we agreed I'd go without Julienne the one-time drummer who had no singing voice and no desire to join a choir. It was four years into our relationship and I'd be gone a month. We'd only ever spent more than a few days apart.

## Other lands—three: let the chorus begin

Sydney-based singer and composer Tony Backhouse specialised in American gospel musical traditions. I loved all the music that came out of those traditions from blues to soul to jazz and rock 'n' roll, and I was so excited to joining one of his USLA tours. I would be joining like-minded choristers assembled specifically for the purpose of visiting and singing with African-American churches and choirs across the country.

We started out in Los Angeles where an irritating chemical tinge pinked the air. Our choir was a motley lot ranging from semi-professional singers to ordinary choristers like myself to some that had more enthusiasm than ability. Most were from Australia, but some came from Europe and the UK. It wasn't until we landed in LA that we all came together and crammed long practice sessions into a very short time frame before we went 'on the road'. Most non-African Americans did not generally experience what we were about to. Anyone could technically enter any church and be welcome but the memory of those Jim Crow years, particularly in the South, lingered and kept the races culturally apart. I wasn't a church-going person and had renounced my Catholic upbringing, but I was more than willing to experience the music. We couldn't sing and move like the locals but with a few good soloists and some original gospel pieces penned by Tony Backhouse, along with encouragement from those in the pews, we rocked as well as a bunch of non-African Americans could.

I was walking well, having had both hips replaced and one revised, and I hit the ground fast. Adrenalin was my friend. We stayed in a beautiful hotel in the French district of New Orleans and scoured the local jazz joints and open markets. I went to live shows featuring B. B. King, Sonny Rollins, the Neville Brothers and the Blind Boys of Alabama.

In Birmingham, Alabama, churchgoers wore the kind of finery one preserved for weddings—fancy hats, lots of lace and funky suits. This was despite the poverty we observed in the dilapidated neighbourhoods. The religious culture shock was immediate. One didn't simply go to church, one 'did' church with conviction with preachers who riffed like hip-hop artists along with the most energetic gospel singing accompanied by drums, organ and electric guitars and microphones.

*'I'm too HAPPY to be SNAPPY! I'm too BLESSED to be STRESSED!'*

Those of us who had experienced Christian church services in Australia could barely compare this to the weak hymns in four-by-four time along with the dull sermons that may have been pious but rarely embodied anything like enthusiasm.

We passed the 16th Street Baptist Church bombed by members of the Ku Klux Klan in 1963, in which four African-American girls were killed. The echoes of segregation were everywhere. In the lobby of the Birmingham Civil Rights Institute, an enormous black and white photo of a little girl sitting on Martin Luther King Jr's lap welcomed us. Serendipity had us meeting that young girl, now a middle-aged woman, who happened to be visiting the Institute that day. She encouraged us to sing gospel with her in the lobby. Seeing this woman grinning up at her little self, with the father of the civil rights movement whose image had been taken only days before his assassination, cemented a moment that more than spoke to anything beyond that lobby.

I walked the streets of New York with a confident stride so as not to look like a vulnerable tourist—so much so that a car full of Americans pulled over and asked me for directions. At a progressive church in Harlem our choir sang with the Addicts Rehabilitation Center Gospel Choir, a group of African-American men and women being supported and uplifted through community singing. They towered over me like tree trunks and sang with great strength and conviction.

I went to the classy Carlisle Hotel on Manhattan's Upper Eastside with someone who had a loose connection to the crooner, Tony Bennett. We were invited to his table. He bought me a glass of champagne. He then stood up and gave an impromptu performance in recognition of the pianist, whose sleek black grand piano had become covered in bouquets. The woman, of indiscriminate age, whose long dyed red hair was pulled up so far it gave her an instant facelift, was playing her final night after a twenty-year residency.

I experienced so much in that short couple of weeks travelling through the US it could have been a year. I walked for miles and felt stronger and fitter than I'd ever been. I was all muscle.


### Julienne and the season of sunflowers—two

Doors slid open and passengers spilled out crumpled and exhausted from the long flight. I'd had the best time but spent half the flight with my eyes clogged with conjunctivitis and just wanted to get home. I collapsed into Julienne's arms, so grateful she was there to pick me up from the airport. But as she grabbed my luggage from the carousel I sensed something about her had changed.

A few mornings later we woke to the sun streaming through lace curtains. Her breath, normally sweet, smelled like stale milk. She pulled back the bedclothes and I commented on a distinctive lump on her right breast.

'I reckon you should get that checked out,' I said.

'It's probably just another one of my cysts,' she said.

'Will you go and check it out just for me?'

'Okay, just for you.'

A few days later she was walking to the bathroom and I commented that her stomach looked swollen.

'Do you have any pain?' I asked.

'I feel just fine,' she said, 'don't be a worry wart!'

A week later she stood in the doorway of my office where I worked as a mental health resource worker for Carer Support Services at the Bendigo Healthcare Group.

'It's not a cyst,' she said, leaning into the door frame for support.

It was breast cancer and the lump was an aggressive two-centimetre anomaly that had to be excised. When they performed the lumpectomy they also took lymph nodes from under her arm to check whether it had metastasised. Her lymph nodes were clear.

We celebrated by bringing in the year 2000 with fireworks and the honking masses partying in Melbourne's CBD. New century. Fresh start.

A few weeks on, after a cafe lunch in Brunswick, Julienne leaned on a parked car and vomited into the gutter. My breaky bones held fast but my guts twisted with a knowing I didn't want to face. My beloved was seriously ill.

The X-rays illuminated on the wall meant little to us but spoke volumes to the oncologist who stood, tapping a finger to his lips.

'I'm afraid the cancer has metastasised. The nausea you are experiencing and the pains in your chest are a result of calcium leaching from your ribs into your bloodstream.'

Her bones were literally dissolving. Those clear lymph nodes had just been a couple of the lucky ones. I gently took her hand to steady both of us. The air left the room and I felt sucked into a black hole where time felt reduced to a dot.

We asked questions but we couldn't take in the answers. Had the sense of impending doom Julienne was experiencing when we'd first met been a premonition?

An MRI exposed further ravages. Julienne's liver was so full of tumours it looked like a bratwurst sausage. She had spots on her lungs. Her spine was disintegrating. Chemotherapy might give her some time, but we weren't going to grow old together. Further tests confirmed Julienne had inherited the BRCA (breast cancer) gene. Several of her female relatives had also contracted breast cancer but to date no one in the family had actually died from it. Julienne had been careful to have yearly mammograms and less than twelve months prior to her diagnosis no lump had been detected.

Three weeks before she died, her five female cousins visited for the last time. As children they had been as close as sisters. Cousin Kay, a film and TV producer, naturally brought her recording equipment. That weekend Julienne lost her hair and finalised her funeral plans.

The day Julienne was hospitalised for the last time she handed me a silver necklace I'd given her for safekeeping. I put it in a pocket of my leather jacket and walked to the car with a brick in my throat. The horizon was a deep orange, the few clouds streaked pink. It was the end of summer and I knew by the time I got back to the cottage it would be dark and there'd be a chill in the air.

Come on kiddo, you'd better get used to it, this being alone business …

As I unlocked the door I felt in my pocket and it was gone. Julienne's necklace had snaked its way through a hole in the lining. It wasn't in the car or the driveway. Gone!

I walked into the dark lounge room and fell on all fours. I heard a sound like a wolf howling for its mate. Then a voice came through: *You knew. You knew all along this was going to happen. This is why you are here.*

I spent the next day scouring florists for out-of-season sunflowers. Wouldn't I prefer a fresh autumn spray? No! They were sentimental, I said. They were symbolic. I was given quizzical looks, but no one pushed me further. Florists, I imagined, were used to quirky requests for elusive blossoms and stalks. The bunch I was eventually handed were miserable runts but the bald-headed grin from Julienne made them grow. Once they were displayed in a vase, she looked wistfully to the gum tree outside and said, 'I look at leaves differently now.' For the first time I felt her path gently peeling away from mine. I could follow only so far.

Julienne wanted to die at home and I made it happen. Her bones were too fragile to sleep in a normal bed so she lay in the dining room in an overstuffed hospital chair-bed from where she could see the lounge and kitchen and beyond to her beloved cottage garden where she had worked almost every weekend, usually topless, if not naked. Julienne hated wearing clothes, much to the horror of the Baptist churchgoers next door. At the end of the day we'd sit out back, wine in hand, and admire the roses, the garden beds and her vegetable patch. 'Ah, ya wouldn't be dead for quids,' she'd say as we watched the sun set over Mount Tarrengower.

Mum and my aunt Claire came and stayed for a bit. Julienne fell into a coma and we were told she would be gone in the next twenty-four to forty-eight hours. The three of us decided to take a short break and drive the twenty minutes to Castlemaine for lunch. We were still waiting for our order when the call came through to get back quick. Julienne took her last breath two minutes before we made it through the door. I'd like to think she'd timed it that way.

Kay turned the weekend of the cousin's reunion into a documentary called *Celebrating Julienne*. Our story travelled round the world and picked up a few awards along the way. It is still being used as an educational tool for medical staff. Julienne is so alive in her dying—funny, brave, and accepting.

She had only three months to live after her diagnosis and in that time I saw her cry only once. From then on, Julienne took it upon herself to square with everyone she knew and loved, planned her funeral to the last minute and gave me a million goodbyes. We even had a wake in our backyard while she was still alive. 'I don't want everyone to have a party without me,' she said, 'we won't call it a wake—we'll call it a wide-a-wake!'

A few years on and two of the five cousins (including Kay) have also succumbed to the BRCA gene and are no longer with us. Fuck cancer! Often, on the edge of sleep, I see Julienne walking down a dusty lane. She turns momentarily and waves, then continues on into the distance.


### Other lands—four: don't kiss the Blarney Stone!

After Julienne died, I collapsed from exhaustion. For the last three months my goals, my sense of purpose had been inextricably linked with a person who now existed only in object and memory. I traced my fingers over everything she had touched. I stood in her garden as autumn settled over everything she'd tended. I returned to work briefly but was told to take more time when my boss found me wandering the corridor, unaware of the tears streaming down my face. I went and stayed with a relative of Julienne's in San Remo. They had a made a spare bedroom in their basement garage and it was there on the indoor steps leading to the garage that I slipped and fell, instantly fracturing my left femur. The paramedics drove me to a local footy oval where an ambulance helicopter was waiting to fly me directly to the Alfred Hospital.

No one expected I would want to return to Julienne's cottage where I'd be fending for myself on crutches, my leg internally wired and wrapped in a brace, but there was nowhere else I imagined I could be. The cottage needed me. Julienne's knick-knacks, her clothes, her books, her paintings, her pots and pans needed me.

It was an icy winter. Friends and neighbours stoked my wood fire and kept an eye on me but I was distant, numb, a shadow barely aware of the comings and goings. The commitment ring Julienne put on my finger turned black.

By spring I was physically healed. I ventured into Julienne's garden and attempted to mow the grass. Trying to get her old petrol lawnmower working broke two of my ribs. The veggie patch went to seed. Sulphur-crested cockatoos deflowered the almond tree. The resident blue-tongue lizard sunned itself on the unused barbecue. I sat in the garden with a bottle of wine as the sun set over Mount Tarrengower and yelled at the sky, 'Ya wouldn't be dead for quids!'

2002. My savings for our planned trip to Europe sat unused. Then Su, a fellow member of the a cappella group *Mama's Chocolate Box* I'd joined the year before, invited me to go to Ireland with her. She'd been saving a while and was keen to check out the music scene over there, as well as 'get in touch with her roots'. She just needed a travelling companion who had the time and the money to accompany her. I figured Ireland was as good as anywhere else, and also part of my ancestry. I could see the world afresh and shake off part of my grief under northern skies.

Just before we were to leave I developed pain in my right thigh. An X-ray didn't reveal any fractures but what it did expose was a slight bend in the bone. Everything was planned and booked and my body inconvenienced me most days so I just pushed through and included in elbow crutches and painkillers to my luggage. For added insurance I managed to get hold of an external electromagnetic bone stimulator, which was an expensive contraption I strapped to my thigh for a few hours each day to enhance bone healing.

Had there not been a hire car I wouldn't have managed much of the trip. Despite appearing as a 'normal' tourist in photos taken sans crutches and bone stimulator, every day was more painful than the last. It didn't help there was so much rain that even our hooded raincoats couldn't keep us from becoming saturated. The gale winds coming off the Atlantic and the force of horizontal downpours had us looking for the nearest pub with a roaring fire, home-made apple pie and Irish coffee to keep us warm. I could never have imagined such wintry blasts coming at us in what was their summer.

The fitness of my free-walking days in the US fell away as I struggled to keep up with Su through rocky outcrops, ancient cemeteries and stone castles. My upper body increasingly took the weight of my failing leg. This didn't hold me back from successfully taking on the hundred spiral steps of Blarney Castle, the medieval stronghold in County Cork. The view from the top was wonderful—not so much the hunched old man whose job it was to wipe the Blarney Stone with his dirty rag after every tourist 'kissed' it for good luck. Managing to get to the top of Blarney Castle on crutches without stumbling backwards was luck enough for me.

I was constantly torn between taking in the beautiful country-side and wanting to lie in a dark room. I could see Su was getting frustrated with me but there was nothing I could do or say that could improve the situation. By the time we'd crossed into Northern Ireland, with its soldiers and guns at the border, and gazed across the Northern Channel to Scotland from the cylindrical rocks of the Giant's Causeway, I needed to find a hospital.

I was grinding my teeth with the pain in my leg. Whatever the external bone stimulator was meant to do, it wasn't working. The hospital doctor eventually prescribed opioids but not before raising her eyebrows over me doing an overseas trip on elbow crutches. How could I explain that I wasn't going to ruin Su's holiday plans and sacrifice the possibility of an adventure because, with my body, there's never really a right way or a right time to travel? I organise what I can then jump on plane and hope for the best.

Su took on all the driving as I sat in a happily drug-fuelled haze. I gazed giddily out at the ocean crashing against the Cliffs of Moher and picked my way over The Burren, a vast moonscape of limestone where wildflowers are harvested and turned into unique fragrances at the Burren Perfumery. In Ballyvaughan we traipsed through the dark recesses of the Aillwee Cave system. Water dripped overhead and on to the slippery stone floors. I moved slowly, sliding my feet and crutches forward like a cross-country skier, as Su paved the way with her torch. The cave was full of hibernation pits carved by bears extinct for at least a thousand years. It wasn't until we re-emerged from the cave into the light that I discovered the moisture on my face was tears. I couldn't help but envisage those bears snuggling down for the winter only to re-emerge each spring, weak and starving, to find less and less food and less and less forest and more and more hunters at the ready until all that was left were the sunken resting places they had dug with their own bear claws.

Against the backdrop of history there were new housing estates popping up everywhere and roundabouts imitating Celtic spirals, which were frightening to navigate with some accommodating up to seven lanes of traffic. Everywhere local pubs overflowed with World Cup enthusiasts and thick layers of cigarette smoke parted to reveal people so drunk that one man in Wicklow thought I was related to 'the girl down the road.' A comedian from the US, who performed at an international comedy festival in the medieval town of Kilkenny, pointed out as he sucked on a pint that, 'In any country I'd go to detox. Here I could live among you.'

Back home, a fracture was confirmed and, as with my left femur, the bend had to be straightened and the leg braced with bone from the bone bank. Of course, the leg would eventually heal but my heart still pained with the loss of Julienne and I had no timeline for that.

The bone that was wrapped around my femur came from a young man who'd lost his life in a motorbike accident. His forearm was the perfect size for my leg.

# NAVIGATING
# PERSPECTIVE

**Bag of poison: pure paranoia**

2003. A dull glare shafts through the bag hooked high on a metal pole. I watch the clear saline laced with antibiotics slipping into my veins, steady, slower than a pulse. Air flutters through a vent in the wall. The surgery has left me confused, unmoving, exhausted. I've been here so many times it all runs together, this chrysalis body of mine reshaped and reinvented a hundred times over.

Yesterday I also had blood dripped into me this way. I'd lost so much in surgery that the pink in my lips and cheeks had become alabaster. The bag of blood looked dark crimson, almost black. It is a strange feeling, seeing someone else's life force flowing into me. A swirling mix of necessity, gratitude and revulsion: the vampire's curse. While the foreign blood fed me, I began to wonder what might be being transferred, despite the strict screening. I am the medium-rare blood type AB+, scarce and much coveted. Before the surgery I went to the blood bank to donate to myself—an autologous transfusion—but I felt like an imposter getting all the attention and the free drinks and chocolate bars regular donors receive for volunteering their blood in the name of altruism or a break from the office. And I was a failure at taking on the frighteningly large 16-to-17-gauge needle used to drain the half litre required. It is a big needle for a big vein, usually in the crook of the arm: the go-to vein. Mine are scarred from overuse. The nurse struggled to get a hundred or even fifty millilitres drained from me. My thickened walls resisted the pressure and when my sorry veins felt the needle about to break into the stream, they rolled away and collapsed because all those cells have memories— millions of cells firing, remembering. Intelligent circuitry. Every one of my cells holds the experience of fluids sucked out and fluids shoved in. And they don't like it.

I am woken by a cold flush. Infusions are never warm. How long have I slept? Through the window the sky looks unchanged but the kitchen has left afternoon tea on the bedside table. The saline bag has reduced to two-thirds. I smell a strange, chemical odour from my pores and a taste of metal on my tongue. It has me wondering if this saline, clear as fresh water, is carrying something other than prescribed antibiotics.

The wondering becomes panic. I immediately think of That Woman, that poor woman, who went to hospital to have a baby. The epidural, needled into her spine. When did she feel it, that chlorhexidine swill? How quickly did it surf into her grey matter, destroy nerves, paralyse her from the feet up? A surface compound, antibacterial, to be swabbed near openings, open wounds, incisions, swabbed to clear the skin before a needle is inserted. It was a simple mistake. A sealed plastic bag of clear fluid of similar viscosity, undetectable by scent.

I'm convinced this infusion is dripping poison second-by-eternal-second. There is a label stuck to the bag but it's too far away for me to decipher.

It's not as if my body hasn't rejected medications before. Some antibiotics give me stomach cramps, morphine gives me skin rashes, another painkiller gave me weeping red skin, hair and muscle loss and the beginnings of organ failure. I'd earned my state of hysteria.

I rip off the tape and unravel the bandage that secures the cannula deep in my arm. I look at the tube of fluid it's connected to. Do I press the buzzer for a nurse? When do I press the buzzer? They'll think I'm being hysterical. But mistakes are made all the time in hospitals. Mistakes rarely made public. An unfortunate death. Cover-ups. Medical bodies too powerful to be sued unless there are headlines.

I don't want to be a cover-up or a headline.

I buzz for a nurse. The patient brochure notes they should respond within two minutes but no one is coming. It's handover time when staff are short on the ground and I'm not a priority. I'm well past the post-operative twenty-four-hour monitoring.

The buzzer slips from the shiny bedcover to the floor. I can't reach it. It's connected to the wall beyond the metal pole. Where's the bed adjuster? It's amongst the sheets. I lower the bed as far as it will go and flatten myself out, holding onto the metal bedhead with one hand and spidering the other across the carpeted the floor. I still can't reach.

Should I rip the cannula out of my arm? Should I bellow? I'm too far from the nurses' station for anyone to hear me.

I feel the blood pumping at my temples, only too aware that the faster I breathe, the faster my pulse races, the quicker the poison will be delivered. I've never pulled a needle out before. I could damage the skin. I could infect myself with bacteria from my own hands. And the infusion would continue to drip, drip everywhere, all over the bed and the floor. Cold perspiration stings my forehead.

A nurse comes through the door. 'What can I do for you?'

'I'm scared this infusion isn't right. Can you check the bag. I'm scared it's poisoning me.'

The nurse strolls to the bag. I can see her eyes attempt to give nothing away but they are unbelieving.

'Well, everything's looking as it should be. You're getting the right antibiotics.'

'But what if they were labelled incorrectly? What if the saline isn't really saline? Something feels wrong. It smells wrong. I'm being poisoned!'

Hot tears hit my cheeks. I need fresh air, but the windows are sealed. Outside the day is fading. The nurse flicks on the light and I'm bathed in fluorescence. I'm caught, a butterfly needled to a rubber mattress. I want to be swaddled and released all at once, the flight-and-fight at odds with my body forced against its natural inclinations. It wants to run, hair swept in the wind. It is a constant dream. That, and standing beneath the shadow of a cresting wave poised, tall as building, from which I always wake the moment before it crashes over me.

'Please, please, TAKE IT OUT!!' I lunge at the cannula tethering me to this torture.

'Stop! Okay, okay, I've stopped the fluid. See, I've turned the drip off.' She walks over and takes my hand. 'It's okay, just take a few slow, deep breaths.' But terror demands fast-and-shallow or no breath at all. 'Now, what I'm going to do is go and get another bag of saline and fresh antibiotic solution. Will that help?'

I lock eyes with her and nod. She carefully separates the tubing and wheels it all away. I release a breath I didn't know was still in my chest. The nurse returns with fresh fluids and tubing.

'See? This bag says saline, and this one is the correct antibiotics.'

I nod once, and my eyelids droop. I surrender to the rubber mattress and plastic-coated pillows and the floating dream of a clean salty ocean nudging me to a safer shore.

## Walking on shaky ground: I could have given birth to my own hip

My body and brain have developed a slightly unusual connection when it comes to registering pain and any other physical sensation requiring attention. I'm so used to blocking out the worst of my pain that when my body is sending me messages I should be listening to I don't always consciously pick up on them. At other times I can even block out the effect of painkillers, which means they give me little relief and sometimes my brain can't block out the pain any more and I feel it more keenly than I should. Chronic pain can really play with a body's natural warning signals.

Chronic pain, for the record, is constant recurring pain that lasts more than three months. Pain clinics are designed to deal with managing chronic pain. I have been referred to a few. One clinic diagnosed me with 'central sensitisation'. This is where the nervous system develops a 'persistent state of hyperactivity' and consequently produces amplified pain. The clinic decided I needed to take up meditation, relaxation and breathing techniques as well as hydrotherapy. Their reasoning being that, if chronic pain cannot be minimised, then one can trick the brain into interpreting pain signals as 'safe' rather than a warning that part of your body is ailing or in danger. The problem was that I have practiced all of these for years as well as hypnosis, Alexander technique, Feldenkrais, remedial yoga, massage and acupuncture. I may well have been one of their most 'pro-active pain management patients' before I even turned up on their doorstep. Unsurprisingly, the specialists at the clinic were stumped as to how they could help me.

I have come to the conclusion that I don't necessarily have an 'overreactive central nervous system' at all—in fact, sometimes I do feel pain over large parts of my body and that it is an accurate reflection of what my body is experiencing. I have fluctuating pain centres in my body, which I like to put down to my body moving the pain around so it doesn't hang about too long in any one area. How smart is that? I believe my natural coping mechanisms have resulted from my body experiencing ongoing pain from birth— or even earlier.

Most people with chronic pain have acquired their pain following an accident or medical calamity. Their nervous systems are not used to dealing with chronic pain and they can therefore go on to experience pain as a condition separate from the original cause, which means they continue to feel pain well after the original source of the pain has been rectified. This is what can lead to so-called 'central sensitisation'. Their bodies have the memory of feeling little or no ongoing pain prior to whatever disaster they have experienced so that when the pain arrives their coping mechanisms are not as developed as someone familiar with pain. I am not a medical specialist and this is only what I have surmised based on my own experience because there is no medical data to date that can support my theory. In fact, there is a 'paucity of evidence examining chronic pain in children and adolescents' except to note that 'the available literature suggests that older patients have a higher prevalence of chronic pain than younger groups of patients.' Well, tell me something I don't know! Even car parts start to wear out over time.

Based on my experience, pain clinics are best suited to those with chronic pain acquired later in life. Such patients often become addicted to painkillers as a way of coping and pain clinics often deal with addiction by weaning patients off these drugs while providing alternative treatments including cognitive behavioural therapy as well as all the other therapies I have mentioned. These clinics are not set up to deal with acute pain which, due to my condition, I can also acquire at any moment. Chronic pain and acute pain are difficult dance partners and one can often be confused for the other. Which one is leading? Which is following? I walk on shaky ground.

Of course, I use painkillers myself but I'm careful with them. I only take pain relief and related medications such as muscle relaxants to give me breathing space, to interrupt the 'pain cycle'. What is the pain cycle? Imagine your clothes swishing about in a faulty washing machine that, instead of cleaning your clothes, makes them more soiled. Your clothes represent your body and the dirt they carry is your pain. As your clothes tumble around in the washing machine, they take on the immediate consequences of pain: anxiety, depression, fear, increased perception of pain, etc. Further along in the washing cycle the ongoing pain causes (swish, swish, swish) activity avoidance, progressive de-conditioning, pain with decreasing activity, further activity avoidance. It's a downward spiral, just like the water gurgling in a faulty washing machine that ruins your clothes instead of cleaning them. (This may be a poor analogy but it is my analogy and I'm sticking to it!) People caught in this cycle can end up in a paralysing mess of addiction and crippling health. As we know from the opioid crisis, the more one uses, the more one needs, the greater the risk to overall health, even death. Opioids, which are one of the strongest forms of pain relief, work by depressing the nervous system. Take too much and the body forgets to breathe.

When I'm at home and in control of my own pain management, instead of increasing the dose exponentially, I choose at times to wean myself back to smaller doses. This works to increase the effectiveness of a smaller dose rather than continually upping the ante. Occasionally I even temporarily stop pain medication altogether to check in with myself so I can reconnect with my body's sensations without the numbing effect of medication. I'm in this for the long haul. But still, my body can play tricks on me.

This particular story illustrates my impressive (and sometimes dangerous ability) to block out pain:

In 2006, when I was working in a full-time management job in Melbourne, I noticed I was feeling a little insecure getting about on my two legs. It was as if I was literally walking on eggshells. At this point in my life I didn't need any aids to get around but after a few days I came to work with elbow crutches to steady myself. At no point however, did I feel an increase in pain. A few days later I continued on, ignoring a slight tingling in my groin. I just put it down to my crooked hips. One evening after work, I drove to a friend's house and plonked on her couch as we caught up over a cuppa. I began to feel quite tired. As I got up to leave, the tingling in my groin turned into a nerve reaction that travelled down my whole leg. That's a bit weird, I thought. By the time I got to the door my leg was telling me it wasn't a good idea to put any weight through it. I hobbled to my car, waved goodbye to my friend and drove home. By the time I got to my place I knew something was seriously wrong. The pain wasn't overwhelming but I was suddenly scared to move. It was a strange feeling of being somewhat unhinged. I parked the car in the street and phoned my then partner, Carolyn.

'Can you come out to the car? I think you need to drive me to the hospital,' I said.

I was still in the driver's seat when she came out but I managed to gingerly make my way over the automatic shift and settle into the passenger seat so she could take control. Carolyn drove me to the hospital where I have had most of my surgeries done.

Once at the hospital I requested a wheelchair to take me into emergency, just to be on the safe side. Then I waited calmly with every other patient in the waiting room. Finally X-rays were taken, a fracture was confirmed and I was admitted to the orthopaedic ward. Here we go again …

The next day my orthopaedic surgeon came rushing in looking more alarmed than I felt. He told me that I had seriously fractured my acetabulum (the hip socket to you and me) and my metal hip joint had almost completely broken through my pelvis. Crikey!

I could have given birth to my own hip, I quipped, though no one else thought that was funny.

Delicate surgery was required to re-line my hip socket with bone acquired from the bone bank. My pelvis lacks bone mass and my socket was painfully thin. On the X-ray I could see that the space between my hip joint and my pelvic cavity was like a slip of paper. No wonder it ended up fracturing.

Scientists have recently discovered a new pain-suppression centre in the brain. In the quest for more effective, non-addictive treatments for chronic pain, Dr Fan Wang and his team at Duke University, North Carolina, looked for regions in the brain that were activated by anaesthetics rather than looking for a pain relief centre in the brain. This counterintuitive approach led to the amygdala—that almond-shaped part of the brain found in the temporal lobe responsible for processing memory, decision-making and emotional responses. Research on mice discovered a group of neurons in the central region of the amygdala that, when activated, can suppress the response to painful stimuli. The neurons' connections to other parts of the brain can also project to more than twenty other brain regions involved in sensory and emotional aspects of pain. Dr Wang states, 'Our work raises the possibility that tapping into the power of this internal analgesic system could be an effective alternative to opioids for relieving chronic pain.'

Has my amygdala been doing this pain suppression thing all along? It would explain my ridiculous ability to subconsciously block pain signals. It certainly feels like my body has created some sort of coping mechanism which, even then, can sometimes be overwhelmed and collapses in on itself.

## Mind how you go: a cricket in a matchbox resting its antennae

Anaesthesia is the coma from which most of us return. There is the moment before one passes out and the moment one wakes and the expanse in between is only registered by the clock on the wall. This slip of time is our wormhole, a reminder that the temporal is only one note in a symphony.

2007. My body lies deep, beyond sense, by medication, post-surgery fatigue, the feeling that I'm present but not there. Yet again I have been fashioned into something different but, like a chrysalis, not yet fully formed. My awareness is couched in a kind of muffled darkness—a hibernation waiting until the conditions are right to return. What do the tubes and machines record? My heart still beats, the pulse is slow yet steady, I continue to breathe.

To an observer I am simply a sleeping patient in a hospital bed in recovery. One of rows and rows and rooms full of us. But what small miracles are occurring? How do we right ourselves, our physical bodies, and bring the rest—psyche, soul, ether—into alignment? Protection is required lest one surfaces with fault lines.

My mind is reduced to a small safe space. A tiny sense of self kept alert. The cricket in a matchbox resting its antennae. A Zen to avoid unfettered panic. It is difficult to trust memories, memories that secure us in our self-sense but are slippery as pearls. Our thoughts can make a nonsense of time, our senses a nonsense of reality. When the whole thing becomes elastic, what do we grasp to steady ourselves?

*A woman married a wealthy man who liked to paint. When they travelled, they took many photos and, on their return, placed them carefully in albums as proof of where they'd been: a seaside, a castle, a church. The man took scenes from the photos, painting them in oils and acrylics. After a time, the scenes began to morph and grow more abstract as* his Alzheimer's took hold. He kept on painting, it kept him tethered. Once the walls were filled, a whole room was set aside for storage. He painted as his wife faded before him, became his mother, his long-dead sister. Then he stopped and lost his moorings altogether. The wife, grieving yet relieved that she no longer had the burden of caring for him, spent her husband's wealth on beautiful clothes, though she rarely went out. The paintings, lined in deep rows on the floor became hidden under piles of shopping. She bought enough food to feed a large family though they'd never had children. When her fridge could take no more, she purchased another and set it up in the garage. She took to sitting up late at night with a bucket of ice cream in front of the TV. She would wake up, dawn breaking through the curtains, TV still on. She began to exist in dream states of oxygen deprivation as the CPAP machine gathered dust in her bedroom and sleep apnoea took an ever-greater hold. Voices from the TV became intruders hiding in the walls. People lived in the spare rooms though there was no room for beds, filled as they were floor to ceiling with boxes of toiletries.

I had been this woman's case manager, assisting her to stay at home with the necessary supports to maintain independence. The job was a precarious balancing act, a liminal dance between vitality and demise. She was assigned to me when the stench of rotting food wafted beyond her fence line. There were no living relatives, no friends to speak of, just an overstuffed house no longer functioning as a home. I arranged for her to go into care. She adjusted happily, sitting in front of the enormous TV in the communal lounge room of the nursing home, seemingly under the impression that nothing had changed. What her mind was relaying was a mystery to everyone but her. Problems only arose when she refused to go to her room because how on earth could she when it was full of bicycles?

Before her house was sold, I returned with the task of collecting mementos for her forever room. State Trustees and commercial cleaners would deal with the rest. I went to the photo albums and something turned in me as I looked through scenes from a private life I was never privy to. Scenes from long ago holidays and people long gone. Nothing had been marked, no signs of the journey, just capsuled moments no longer meaning anything to anyone. I stared into the photos and thought of that truth-line from photographer Diane Arbus, 'a photo is a secret about a secret.' I took one from the pile, hoping it would trigger a spark of recognition in her. I went through some of her husband's paintings and chose two that were pleasing to me. I took a vase I thought she might like as well as a couple of other trinkets and closed the door behind me. I left with a mixture of deep sadness and existential fear. Where do memories go when they no longer have a home? How do we ever know what's real when our minds are tethered to the fragility of a human brain? Who are we when we no longer know who we are?

The cricket in the matchbox stirs its antennae, a stretch into the darkness. Before I let the light in, I feel the jarring sting of the knife-wound reminding me where I have been and what has been done. Tomorrow, all being well, my feet will dangle over the bed and I will rediscover the equilibrium of a re-gathered self.

# ADVENTURES
# WITH ALICE

## That sexy garage girl: I adored Miss Anderson

2008. Dexter, my black and silver mini schnauzer, sat buckled up in the back seat of my company car as I pulled up outside the redbrick house in Camberwell. Dexter had been here many times before and he wagged his stumpy tail when Mary cracked open the door. 'Dexter!' she cried, then looked up at me with a blank smile. Mary was in her late eighties and had Alzheimer's. I was her case manager helping her to stay living at home while she could, but we were getting to the pointy end. She always remembered Dexter the de facto therapy dog, but I had become a stranger. She was losing weight, forgetting to eat and she had begun to live in the past as if the present was a waking dream.

I followed her through to the large rear garden where she spent most afternoons tending her plants. Once again, I listened to stories of her time nursing wounded soldiers in Borneo during the war. As she cut flowers to take inside her eyes welled with tears as she re-lived the terrible injuries and the young men crying for their mothers as they took their last breaths. Mary had two sons, now with families of their own, and her Jewish husband had died years before. During the war he'd survived vicious Nazi-trained dogs chasing him through forests and across several

European borders. In suburban Melbourne he'd been terrified every time a dog barked. I wondered what he would have made of Dexter sniffing around in his backyard, which had grown to forest proportions, its tall trees and overgrown shrubs casting long shadows.

I followed Mary into her kitchen, which was full of empty jars, cups and plates, the light from its cracked window struggling to enter through dust and cobwebs. I'd learned not to suggest a tidy up as the clutter seemed to give her comfort. No doubt an occupational therapist would deem Mary's kitchen and other parts of her house a safety risk. However, I'd spent long enough in the business to know that altering anything could further confuse a person with dementia and put them at even greater risk than leaving the risks untouched. I had, though, ensured her stove had been disconnected in case she forgot to turn off the gas.

Mary grabbed a jar for the flowers and moved to the sink to fill it with water. Then she froze and suddenly exclaimed, 'You know, my mother was the driver and mechanic in our family. She worked for Alice Anderson.'

'What? Mary, what did you just say?'

Had she read my mind? I told Mary that I'd first discovered Alice Anderson only weeks earlier when reading a biography of Australia's famous landscape designer, Edna Walling. This was just after the Great War and I'd immediately been fascinated by the diminutive, androgynous woman who'd trained women and employed them as drivers, instructors and mechanics in her garage. She should have been a well-known figure but I'd never heard of her and Google revealed little. Perhaps it was partly because she died in 1926, aged only twenty-nine. And here was Mary, a direct connection to her …

'Oh yes … I adored Miss Anderson!' Mary's eyes twinkled. 'Edna Walling was a friend of my mother's. Mother worked for Miss Anderson for eight years until her eyesight got too bad.'

'Do you have any photos of your mother from the garage?'

'No, I don't think so. Mother was very camera shy, very self-conscious ... They all wore the same uniform as Alice: jodhpurs, driver's cap. I think they wore jodhpurs as a protection against being raped ...'

I wanted to extract every little detail from Mary. I had been searching for the elusive Alice Anderson and she was here before me in this little cluttered kitchen in an old brick home in Camberwell in the mind's eye of a daughter of one of Alice's garage girls. What were the chances? To meet someone who'd met Alice early last century was a miracle. Serendipity, fate, a message from the grave, what did it matter? I had so many questions.

'What was Alice like?' I began scribbling notes as Mary reminisced.

'I thought she was gorgeous. She had her hair cut in an Eton crop, just like mother's hair. She was very mannish and very friendly, never took me to task. She was very popular and brainy too. A very happy person.'

Mary then went to her fridge and opened the freezer. 'What on earth is this doing in here?' she asked, pulling at a litre tub of ice-cream.

'Perhaps you bought it and forgot.'

'No, no, I don't even eat ice-cream!'

Dexter scratched at the door. Mary didn't like him being inside so I suggested we go for a short walk.

'Yes, let's go for a walk!' she said enthusiastically. 'We can go down to the shops and get an ice-cream!'

'I thought you didn't eat ice-cream.'

'Whoever told you that?'

A few weeks later the inevitable happened. Mary was found dehydrated and distressed wandering the streets with a roast chicken under her arm. A bed was found for her in aged care the following week and my job was done.

The next weekend, Dexter jumped excitedly out of the car, ran around me then lurched forward. His tangled lead tripped me up and I landed on my knees on the footpath. Damn! My jeans split. I was fine except for a gravel knee, bloody and stinging, and it wasn't until later I noticed my knee wasn't the only thing hurting. I was in the kitchen cooking dinner when I bent down to open the oven door and a sharp pain in my back had me drawing breath. I froze, then relaxed and the pain disappeared. A few minutes later, same thing. Had I sprained a muscle when I fell? But it didn't feel like any muscle pain I'd had before.

An X-ray showed a fractured vertebra. It usually took a much more spectacular tumble than landing on my knees on the footpath to give me a fracture. I'd spent years improving my bone density with infusions so they didn't break as easily as they had in childhood.

My case management job meant not only visiting clients at home but driving some to appointments, which meant shoving and pulling wheelchairs and wheelie walkers in and out of the car. If it had been a simple desk job, I might have been able to go back to work with a back brace but much of the job was physical. I didn't need surgery, but I had to rest until the fracture healed.

### Three months sick leave: I adored Miss Anderson

I read books.

I tried to find out as much as I could about Alice Anderson.

I got permission to visit Mary in the nursing home.

Mary was so tiny now she looked as if she was disappearing into the bed, a baby bird fallen from its nest, wispy and featherless.

'Hello Mary,' I said. One of her eyes half opened at the mention of her name. 'I used to visit you at home and bring Dexter my dog with me.' She didn't stir.

'And the last time you spoke we talked about Alice Anderson.'

'Oh, I adored Miss Anderson!' she cried, attempting to sit up, her eyes suddenly alive. I put an extra pillow behind her back and pulled up a chair.

'Do you remember the first time you met Alice?'

'I first went to the garage with Mother when I was, I think, four years old. I remember Miss Anderson sliding in and out from under the cars … I asked her lots of questions and Mother said, "You mustn't keep asking questions of Miss Anderson, she's taking lots of parts out and needs to concentrate on putting them all back in the right place. Please wait for Miss Anderson to come out from under the car to get some fresh air!" But Miss Anderson didn't mind, she didn't treat children like nuisances … '

Mary told me she initially went to the garage with her mother Nancy because it took time for babysitting arrangements to be put in place. Mary's parents owned an orchard in Mount Waverley but it made very little money, especially after Mary's father returned damaged from World War One. That was the reason Nancy had to get a job.

Mary continued to fade over the next couple of months. Whenever I arrived at the nursing home she was always in bed. I kept my visits short.

'Oh, I adored Miss Anderson! They were simple engines. You opened up the two sides and the engine was just sitting there. I was brought up to not touch it. Mother said Miss Anderson was very strong. She would lift a whole engine out of the bonnet on her own—something it often took two men to do …'

It was like experiencing a bedtime story in reverse, me sitting next to her and Mary revisiting those childhood days, allowing me to step into her remembered past. I'd always been drawn to the 1920s, the era of art deco, cloche hats, flapper frocks, mannish suits and jazz; the sultry movie stars languorously smoking long cigarettes, the motorcars and aeroplanes—a new age of bright young things and post-war freedoms. And now I was becoming obsessed with Alice and the 1920s, imagining the garage full of women in collars, ties, shirts, jodhpurs and peaked caps chauffeuring people in their shiny motorcars as well as offering driving tuition and mechanical repairs. It sounded daring, sexy and exciting. Alice's life story needed to be told and I was beginning to think I was the one to tell it. I took meeting Mary as confirmation. She was the last person alive who'd actually met Alice and here she was giving me the gift of her memories.

'Oh, I adored Miss Anderson! Sometimes she would let me sit in the backseat … I remember a man jumped in once and looked twice at Miss Anderson and said, "Are you a woman or a man?" Miss Anderson smiled and she said, "I'm a woman and you'd best watch your step!" She wouldn't stand any silly business … Alice was a lesbian.'

I'd read that Alice, and many of her women staff, were often mistaken for men or boys but …

'How did you know Alice was a lesbian?'

'Oh, I don't know. It was just something everyone knew.' This wasn't proof that Alice was a lesbian, but it confirmed my suspicions that this was probably the case. I needed to do more research but, as a lesbian myself, it made me all the more interested in Alice's story and her 'garage girls'. In 1920s Melbourne, being lesbian was a private affair and sexuality a private matter. Homosexuality, at the time, was very much 'the love that dare not speak its name'. If there were lesbians working at the garage, how did they survive let alone thrive? Being visible in the public domain must have been a risky business …

'Do you remember any others who worked at the garage besides Alice and your mother?'

Mary smiled.

'Oh, yes, I remember Miss Snell. She was Miss Anderson's friend. I thought her name was Miss *Smell* and mother always had to correct me. I said to Miss Snell, "You don't smell, I'm sorry I thought that was your name,"' Mary laughed to herself.

Each time I visited Mary she seemed a little smaller, sunken, distant. I knew she didn't have long and, apart from wanting to learn more about Alice, I visited to ensure she was being well looked after in the time she had left.

'Here Mary, have a sip of water … Do you remember the last time I came we were talking about Alice Anderson.'

'I adored Miss Anderson.'

'Yes, she sounds like she was an amazing person. I read that she died very young. Do you remember hearing about that?'

Mary frowned. 'I remember waking up one night and hearing mother crying in the kitchen. It was a shock to hear a grown-up cry … after that I began putting things together.' Her eyes filled with tears.

I knew from Mary's birthdate that she would have been only seven years old when Alice died.

The last time I visited Mary she was shivering a little and I put another blanket over her.

'I have to get up. I've got work to do.'

'Mary, you've worked hard all your life. It's time for you to rest and let go if you want to.'

She died a few days later, just shy of her ninetieth birthday.

As Mary lay dying and my spine was healing, we'd shared a world of memory and imagination. She had given me a private glimpse into the world of 1920s female emancipation (and possible lesbian lifestyles) in the form of a motor garage established by a woman barely out of her teens whose life ended tragically and mysteriously at just twenty-nine years old. What more was there to uncover? And where to begin?

## Alice comes to life on a disability pension

2009. I was at the home of historian Dr Mimi Colligan, a tiny, energetic woman in her seventies. Laid out on her round glass table were albums the size of paperbacks and inside were miniature sepia photographs. A magnifying glass was needed to view them in any detail. The first album I picked up had 'Garage Snaps' written in fountain pen in firm, loopy lettering on the cover. On the inside cover was a signature written in the same confident hand: *Alice E. F. Anderson.* It was at this moment that the elusive, somewhat mythical Alice really came to life. Here I was, touching an object that Alice had signed and compiled.

I decided tracking down information on Alice Anderson was a priority. I quit my job. I'd pushed myself hard and I needed to take a break before I collapsed in a bigger heap. The Disability Pension supported me, as it had when I needed it in the past, and allowed me to take my time searching for Alice.

It had taken me a couple of months to track down historian Mimi Colligan. She'd retired and was living in a lifestyle village in a seaside suburb of Melbourne. In the mid-1980s Mimi had written the first definitive article on Alice Anderson since her death six decades earlier. How had Mimi come across this pioneering woman and why had she plucked her from the dust of history? I had so many questions.

I didn't realise I'd been holding my breath until Mimi handed me the magnifying glass and I let out a gasp at the photographs carefully placed in the 'Garage Snaps' album. Before me were images of boyish young women dressed in overalls and chauffeur uniforms taking oil from a stand, having a cuppa break in the courtyard, posing in the garden, and on a picnic tour, of Alice grinning in a pair of breeches, and photos of the garage. Other albums showed a tour of Tasmania and more private photos of vintage cars, trips on unmade roads, activities in the garage replete with garage cat and dog. All had been taken in the 1910s and 20s.

Most were unmarked so that names and places were up for guessing. These tiny, faded private moments of people long dead held immediacy and mystery in equal measure. Playful whispers and echoes from the grave.

When I first began my research I was told by a few knowledgeable people I'd never be able to find enough information to write Alice's biography. Alice had died way back in 1926 at twenty-nine years of age. There'd be no one alive today who had known Alice, let alone met her, and the information I'd discovered in my initial search was certainly sparse. I started to think about Alice's story as historical fiction. But then came Mary who had met Alice, albeit as a very young girl. And then came Dr Mimi Colligan and her collection of photos.

Mimi was initially aware of the existence of Alice Anderson courtesy of her mother who learned to drive at Alice's Kew Garage in the 1930s. Of course, this was close to a decade after Alice's tragic death by a gunshot wound to the head. But the rumours surrounding her death were raw enough to leave an impression on young Mimi. Alice had been fatally wounded in the garage less than a week after returning from an historic trip to Alice Springs in a 1926 Baby Austin. At the time no one, let alone a woman, had managed to drive from Melbourne to central Australia in such a tiny vehicle.

When Mimi was conducting research for her article in the early 1980s, Alice's sisters and quite a few of the 'garage girls' were still alive. Mimi interviewed every woman she could find who was connected to Alice and a couple of the elderly garage girls loaned her their little box brownie photograph albums. I'd seen a couple of poorly reproduced black and white photos in Mimi's published article and that was enough for me to feel that there must be more to uncover. I'd not had the opportunity to meet these women—they were well gone by the time I'd stumbled upon Alice—but Mimi was to be my entrée into their lives. Had Mimi not thought to write her article and conduct the relevant research many details of Alice's life might have disappeared for good. As for the photographs, when Mimi had gone to return the albums to their owners, the women had passed away. A few months later and Mimi may not have received the albums at all and they may have ended up in landfill. Mimi held onto them with the idea that she might do more with Alice's story, but other commitments and distractions took over. Then I turned up on her doorstep.

Over time, Alice's life was revealed to me in all its historical importance. In her teens Alice had envisaged becoming a motor mechanic. This was at a time when motorcars were far from ubiquitous and women were barely learning to drive, let alone wanting to make a living out of peering under the bonnet. Despite limited funds she dreamed of owning her own garage and employing women only. Alice designed her own unique garage, invented the first device to roll beneath a car's chassis, initiated a women's automobile club, developed the first 'once-over' scheduled car service and designed her own 'Anderson Hood' for convertibles.

Delving into history can be fraught with the missed and the missing. There are facts, and then there are those who record those facts. Then there are 'facts' that are not completely factual. Had Alice been a man, she most certainly would have been a household name as a trailblazer, inventor and entrepreneur.

### Gaining traction—three: don't step through that swinging door!

2011. Another fractured femur. (I know!) This time it happened when I was dining with my mother at a local Thai restaurant. It was around the time I was working up to a knee replacement and I was walking with elbow crutches. The restaurant had dim mood lighting with candles on each table. After our meal I hobbled to the ladies' toilet at the rear where there was hardly enough light to read the scrawled 'out of order' message stuck to the door. As I stood there taking in the note and wondering what the alternative might be, one of the waitresses kindly led me to a door further down the back. It was a swing door and, as she held it open for me, I was blinded by a corridor of white tiles flooded in fluorescent lighting. I blinked and stepped forward then heard myself scream. Suddenly I was about-turned sitting flat on the ground with the door pressing into my swelling right thigh. The waitress turned whiter than the tiles and ran off just as Mum rushed towards me in stockinged feet. One of the diners took charge and held the door away from my fracture. Someone else called an ambulance.

I later discovered that there had been a drop in the floor level from the restaurant area to this rear walkway leading to the men's toilets. There was no warning sign and no actual step to speak of, just a few centimetres difference between the restaurant flooring and the corridor separated by the swing door. Had I been walking unaided I still might have tripped but with two crutches attached to my arm I had no hope of breaking my fall.

It is a tricky thing, this bandaging business. 'Just relax', the nurse said. But how in hell do you relax with such a fracture? The biggest bone in the body completely broken in half, two blind ends chaffing, disoriented in muscle.

Surgery would come but until then traction kept my leg stretched so the floating femur, attached to my knee at one end, hip at the other, would stop the snapped bits butting and skirting in a sea of blood vessels.

The figure eight bandage around my calf that secured the traction and kept the tension just right had to be re-done every twenty-four hours.

'Just relax, breathe.'

The slightest muscle twitch had me yelping. Muscles are designed to contract and when a bone is fractured inside a large muscle group, the default response is spasm.

When I knew it was time to redo the bandage, I would whimper like a dog that knows its next beating is coming. A wrestle of prefrontal cortex over brain stem. Oh, to be a Zen monk. How do they do it? I've never had the patience to still my monkey mind. I like my monkey mind. Meditation can make me anxious, make me want to scratch my way out of a hole.

It was a nurse on afternoon shift who tamed me, wounded and trussed and frightened as I was. She broke through: early evenings, after meals, before sleep. We breathed together, slow, deep, hypnotic. It was only her. She'd found a way to unroll the bandage and keep the tension at the same time. With her I could do the impossible. I let go. All the thigh muscles worked against their intention and gave in to the release. She did the perfect figure-eight (infinity) wrap with just the right tightness to keep traction without cutting my circulation.

## Unhinged and walking on my arse

When I wasn't strapped to a hospital bed, I continued to work hard at compiling Alice's story. I applied for grants and fellowships. I was shortlisted but never won. Submissions to publishers require a publishing history but mine was so scant it barely rated a mention. Nevertheless, I submitted and waited. And waited. Months went by. Those publishers who eventually replied found the story interesting but weren't prepared to take it on. No one gave me a reason or told me what I could do to make the manuscript more publishable. I couldn't afford to pay for a professional manuscript assessment, so I kept on working, fine-tuning, killing my darlings.

I spent hours in front of the computer on the second floor of the house I shared with Carolyn, looking up occasionally to view a magpie or a kookaburra resting on a branch of next door's lemon-scented gum. Carolyn would arrive home from work and call for me to come downstairs. Her calling often shook me out of my 1920s bubble or I'd be woken from a sleep I didn't realise I needed waking from. It was 2013, five years since I'd left work to concentrate on the 'Alice Project'. In that time I'd had:

– A plate inserted along my bent left femur, which swelled and then collapsed my knee joint
– A total left knee replacement which, complicated by the joint collapse, meant I could no longer bend the knee more than 80 degrees
– A fractured right femur
– A plate inserted along my fractured right femur, which then fell apart and fractured the bone in two places
– A right hip revision that included a titanium rod that ran inside the length of my femur to replace the failed plate.

That final surgery resulted in a massive post-operative infection that came close to killing me. What was meant to be one surgery became several. I spent a week in ICU on powerful 'last resort' antibiotics, the final frontier against bacterial-resistant strains. I had several surgical 'wash outs' that included the removal of infected muscle and bone. After all that could be done was done, my surgeon hung his head, stating the infection 'had ruined me'. He told me I would never walk again.

But I wasn't finished with walking. A few months later I was housesitting in New South Wales on Oxley Island with Carolyn. The beautiful old house had been part of an old dairy farm and was surrounded by a few acres. From the gate to the house alone was a kilometre long. At this stage I was doing short walks on elbow crutches. With little else to do but read and write, I decided to see how far I could get down that driveway. My schnauzers, Dexter and Alice (named after you-know-who!) and Carolyn's bitzer, Maxwell Tuff, accompanied me each day as a I went little further each time.

It took a couple of weeks, but I finally made it from the house to the gate. The return trip was always a lot slower and one afternoon, less than halfway back to the house, the hovering clouds let loose with a massive downpour. The dogs danced about shaking off the rain as I kept on, wanting to quicken the pace but knowing that slipping in the puddles forming around me could have been disastrous. The temperature plummeted and the cold crept in as my clothes stuck to me and rivulets ran down the back of my shirt. My glasses steamed up and I could hardly see where I was going. Then I made out Carolyn's white car coming towards me.

'What the hell are you doing out in this weather ya crazy woman?'

By the time I and three wet mutts slid into the back seat I was laughing, not caring how soaked I was and relieved I didn't have to wade all the way back.

The next day the sun was out again and soon I made the driveway walk to the gate and back my regular routine. A whole two kilometres of crutch-walking every single day. After four weeks I was strong and walking, still with elbow crutches but with no thought of using a wheelchair. Eventually I got down to a walking stick.

When, after a few months, I sauntered through the door of my surgeon's office on one stick, he was incredulous. He put my stick aside, took my arm and lead me around the room to understand exactly how I was managing to do the almost impossible. I was favouring my 'good' left leg but my right leg that no could longer take weight properly was compensating by over engaging my gluteal muscles. I was literally walking on my arse.

Getting about this way continued to be possible but incredibly exhausting. I often used elbow crutches to make things easier but, even then, every step I took used up to ten times the energy of an able-bodied person's step and my compromised spine was increasingly feeling the strain of yet another way of moving. However, I knew if I stopped trying to walk, I could lose the ability altogether.

Then my right hip dislocated not once, but twice. The muscle that had been removed had clearly destabilised the prosthesis. The first time my surgeon manipulated the hip back into place under anaesthesia and hoped for the best. The second time, in desperation, he fashioned a cup around the joint in the hope of securing it from ever dislocating again. So far so good—but I have to be careful not to bend too far in any direction. If it dislocates again, there is nothing else that can be done. I will be left with a 'floating hip' so damaged by all the surgeries that I certainly will never walk again.

Amongst this revolving door of hospitalisations, the Alice Project was, literally, keeping me alive. It gave me purpose when I had no job prospects, limited physical mobility, mountains and valleys of pain, and the spectre of whatever-the-hell-might-happen-to-me-next. I'd been in contact with Dr Georgine Clarsen, one-time mechanic and academic who'd written her dissertation on early women motorists, one of whom was Alice Anderson. I'd tracked down relatives of Alice and some of her garage girls. This project had developed into something that was no longer a private curiosity. It came with expectations from people close to the story. Obligations were now built into my purpose and I didn't want to let anyone down, least of all Alice herself. I had to keep going.

Daily serves of slow-release opioids had me falling asleep in the middle of typing a sentence. I'd only realise my eyes had been closed once I opened them. I would lose chunks of time this way.

It seemed no matter how much I concentrated on developing Alice's story I was falling backwards, a Sisyphus rolling that enormous boulder up the hill only to have it roll down again. I was failing Alice and my body was failing me. As the light faded each day I could feel myself descending into that dreaded, familiar black hole where hope struggles for air.


## Other lands—five: floating down the Mekong

2016. I couldn't escape the endless cycle of chronic and acute pain made only half bearable by ingesting a constant stream of stupefying medications. I lay in bed and dreamt of caged birds and broken wings.

I rang my mother. I cried. She decided I needed a change of scenery. Suddenly the two of us were booked for a tour of Vietnam. 'I got a cheap deal!' she said. I had no idea how we'd manage. A few years prior Mum had slipped on a carrot in a super-market and shredded a tendon in her foot. Neither of us could walk under our own steam to a corner shop.

In Ho Chi Minh City, masses of motorbikes, cars, buses, three-wheeled cycle rickshaws and pedestrians converged and sped through broad intersections ignoring all traffic lights and road rules. To cross the road was to put your life in danger. Numerous fatalities a day occurred across the country. Lost in a whirling dervish of noise and colour with no rulebook to follow (or at least not rules we understood), Mum and I would hold hands and, eyes half-closed, step off the kerb. The reward for surviving to the other side was a warm foot spa.

We walked along the banks of the Mekong River in the hot sun, traditional conical hats atop our heads. The concrete path leading to the rickety wooden canoes looked like it had been constructed in a wet cement-throwing competition. Two tour guides led us to the edge by our arms. I kept my head down, picking out the flat spaces in which to land my walking stick. There is no elegant way to get into a canoe. My leg with the prosthetic knee that wouldn't bend more than eighty degrees and the other leg that could barely hold weight struggled to find any sort of balance until I'd unceremoniously centred my arse on one of the wooden benches. We had a guide to row. She took a photo of Mum and me peeking out from under our conical hats, smiling for posterity.

A boat in Halong Bay took us amongst the limestone islands and rock caves. We knew not to attempt the long steep trek up to the giant cave bathed in coloured lights. Our camera went with a guide who promised to take photos for us while we waited, contemplating the empty plastic bottles and other pollution bobbing on the beautiful blue-green sea. Poison in Paradise. All those small plastic bottles of water, handed out to tourists on an hourly basis because drinking local water in Vietnam was unsafe.

The Vietnam Military History Museum in Hanoi. Incessant gunshot noise from the range where tourists played with weapons used in the war. The dry, dusty silence inside the Cu Chi tunnels of the underground network built by Vietnamese guerrilla fighters. Vicious spiked traps devised by both enemy and ally displayed in situ, describing the torturous, slow death each would bring. Surrounding jungle eerily still with the echoes of screaming men. We couldn't leave quickly enough.

War fallout as tourism. It was everywhere. Buses paused for toilet stops connected to closed markets with goods created by locals whose bodies were deformed with the effects of Agent Orange. The 'toilet stops' lasted for up to an hour each time. We did our penance, limping past the overpriced stalls where bent, twisted bodies focused on their craft. Look! Look what you have done to us! Pay! Pay for our suffering! We will convert your dollars as you bear witness. Had I been born in Vietnam I doubt I would have survived long enough to suffer such after-effects of war.

## Riding sidecar with Alice

In 2015, I'd set up my aliceandersongaragegirl Facebook page as a blog with photos, stories of discovery and the progress I was making. But as time went on I became increasingly distressed at the delays, the forced time out, the constant re-evaluation. There came a point where I felt I'd set up something I was incapable of finishing. I had an increasing number of Facebook followers: historians, Alice's family members and relatives of garage girls all checking in.

'When's the book coming out?!' It was a constant question I couldn't answer. Eventually I created a message on the Facebook page from Alice Anderson herself who explained some of what was happening to her author and that she, too was frustrated at how long everything was taking.

Meanwhile, even without a book to show for my efforts, interest around Alice was increasing. First, there was a television production company Bombora, who emailed me about accessing some photos of Alice and her garage girls for a documentary on the social history of the car in Australia. They purchased some images and I was acknowledged in the credits of *The Wide Open Road,* which was first featured on ABC-TV in 2011.

Then there was the call from Belfast.

It came out of the blue post-surgery while I was still in hospital doped to the eyeballs. The caller was a BBC-TV producer who was interested in including Alice Anderson in a documentary series the BBC was creating around the Northern Ireland diaspora. Alice's parents were Protestants from Northern Ireland, so this made sense, though I have no idea what I said to the woman. I would have been shocked to receive a call from the BBC no matter what state I was in. Factor in my skewed, drug-addled brain and clouded social filter, I hate to think how the conversation went. I do recall her stating the documentary would not be shown in Australia though she was keen for me to be a talking head. Apparently, I was now the 'world expert' on Alice. Clearly, I was in no state to be interviewed on TV, so I must have made enough sense to direct her towards Georgine Clarsen, who agreed to take my place. A disappointing lost opportunity but the whole process with this Alice Project seemed to be paired with a series of unexpected and vicarious joys. I may have been lying in a half-stupor, but I used this time to dream and believe whatever was happening was all part of a grand plan orchestrated by Alice herself. Alice had been real and she was directing the whole palaver from some celestial cloud. She'd chosen me to write her life story. She was confident I could pull it off. Who was I to question the process? Alice had achieved things many imagined were impossible. Was what I was doing so different? I took the quote from Alice's business card—*Qui n'a risque rien, n'a rien* (nothing ventured, nothing gained)—and held the faith.

# EXTREMUS EVENTUS
## (With the corpus)

**You're going to do … what?**

2017. I'm staring at a metal entanglement on the surgeon's desk. It looks like a metallic scream and I can barely imagine the concept let alone the process.

'Looks mediaeval. An instrument of torture,' I say.

The spinal surgeon turns in his swivel chair and smiles.

'It's the latest technology,' he says.

'How many of these total spinal fusions have you done?' I ask.

'Around 150.'

I suppose that counts for experience.

'Have you ever operated on someone with Osteogenesis Imperfecta?'

No, this surgeon has never operated on someone with my condition.

'But the requirements are the same,' he says. 'You'll need to pass a bone mass and bone density test before we can proceed.'

I ask, as I always do, about surgical risks and his response shocks me. I've been through countless major surgeries on my hips, femurs and knees but apparently they are nothing compared to what's being proposed here.

'The surgeries you've had in the past, they're a two, three, maybe four-out-of-ten. This one's a nine-out-of-ten. The physical recovery is incredibly gruelling.'

So I'm thinking of having surgery that seems to outrank anything else that can be done to a human body and remain breathing.

'The operation takes so long we now do it in two stages,' he says. 'Still, there's risk of vision impairment and dementia.'

Here I was thinking possible nerve damage, paralysis, postoperative infection and suddenly I have to contemplate my head. Apparently, one needs to be facedown on the operating table for up to eight hours and this means a lot of pressure on the eyeballs so capillaries can burst and … okay, scary, makes sense, but the dementia? Well, that's because you have to be under such a deep anaesthetic for so long it can mess with your brain function. So, the payoff for a straighter spine could be going blind and losing my mind.

As I lie in bed at home with a pillow in between my knees to ease my pain, I imagine all that metal in my body. If I do have this surgery, I calculate approximately 50% of my skeleton will be covered by, or replaced with, foreign material. People used to joke about me becoming a bionic woman after that corny 1970s American sci-fi TV show *The Six Million Dollar Man* and its spin-off, *The Bionic Woman* starring Lindsay Wagner. In the show Wagner's character, Jaime Sommers, suffered a nearly fatal accident and was reborn as the first female cyborg. Both of her legs were replaced allowing her to run more than sixty miles an hour and jump off buildings. An arm was also replaced, allowing her to bend steel with her bare hands. But I don't want to be a superhuman cyborg—I don't even expect to be 'normal'. Just let me breathe with less pain, not go blind or lose my mind.

I just have to hope I will pass the required bone mass and bone density test because, despite the risks, I really don't see an alternative. Life with escalating pain and decreasing mobility is no way to live. I must continue a precarious, progressive dance on a metal pin.

From what was a perfectly normal-looking skeleton at birth has, over time, transformed into a twisted pelvis, double scoliosis, malformed sacrum and a lower lumber turned inwards, like a 'C'. The irony is that, until recently, I looked reasonably normal on the outside. Given the necessity, bodies can perform amazing compensations, sort of like a slow-moving party trick.

I turn in the shower to view my back from the bathroom mirror. I can almost see my spine curving and falling apart in real time. The spinal surgeon doesn't believe me when I tell him I can feel, even hear my spine collapsing like faulty scaffolding.

'This process probably took at least two years,' he states. I know what I'm experiencing is galloping with speed and it's terrifying. And how ironic that I have passed the requisite bone mass and density test for this nine-out-of-ten extreme surgery because I have been bolstered by osteoarthritis.

The first operation will have me lying face up. They will take a scalpel to my lower abdomen. They will push my entrails aside and drill four-inch screws into my pelvis. For the second operation I will be lying face down for at least six hours. The skin covering my spine will be sliced open and my spine (exposed and glistening under the lights) will be realigned from sacrum to shoulders with a series of rods and screws. I wonder if there will be a wrenching sound as the surgeons (it's a two-surgeon job) stretch out my inverted C and straighten the two scoliosis curves, one bending left, one right.

I survived the first operation though my fragile pelvis didn't take kindly to those invasive screws and one caused a fracture. The surgeon resolved to fix this at stage two.

After lying face-down in the second operation for eight hours I was wheeled into ICU where everything is quiet and dark except for the beeping and flashing of machines. Some patients don't make it and calmly fade under Code Blue surrounded by staff gathered to attempt a miracle.

I woke lying on my back, fully alert with a tube down my throat. Once the nurse responsible for monitoring me heard my groans she put a button in my hand and told me to press. It was a patient-controlled analgesia (PCA) device that allowed me to self-administer small amounts of pain relief. The PCA is set to pre-prescribed doses at pre-prescribed intervals with pre-prescribed limits to the number of doses that can be received within a certain time frame. PCAs have been proven to reduce the amount of pain relief a patient requires. However, my pain was so off the scale no micro-dosing was going to help.

Finally, the nurse came and dragged the tube from my rasping throat so I could speak. I told her I was in a lot of pain, but she just encouraged me to keep using the PCA. As with all nurses in ICU she was measured and calm. My groans got louder and she came towards the bed. I grabbed her arm with such ferocity she was momentarily startled but quietly told me to take some deep breaths. I wanted to rip her throat out. I'd just had my whole back split open, had rods and screws wrench and realign my spine, which happens to be attached to my ribs, which happen to move in and out when my lungs take in and expel air. It hurt to breathe at all, let alone deeply. I felt like I'd been splayed and nailed to a fence. I couldn't even rock my head back and forth in the soothing way I'd done as a child.

Nurses came and went, occasionally topping up my baseline analgesia but it was never enough to even take the edge off. I faded in and out of consciousness like a victim of torture waiting for the final release. A few times I floated out of my body and across the ceiling before being dumped back on the bed. Finally, I couldn't take it any more.

I crashed through my own pain barrier and screamed H-E-L-P!! Earlier, I would have been embarrassed to disrupt the calm.

I'd been in ICU enough times to know how one's existence relies on everything being controlled with subdued efficiency. Releasing my voice felt like swearing obscenities in church or smashing a Ming dynasty vase. But it was effective. Suddenly staff raced from everywhere to my bedside as if I'd set off my own Code Blue, which in a way I had. Doctors and nurses tried to hush me, but I'd released the beast and couldn't stop.

I must have been knocked out with something because being removed from ICU was a blur. But I do remember being wheeled to the orthopaedic ward and the nurse in charge saying, 'This happens all the time. If you'd come straight here, we would have looked after you.' What?!

It was only once I was out of ICU that I finally received the level of pain relief required. The irony wasn't lost on me that ICU is where a patient is most closely monitored by a dedicated nurse. One is never left alone and all vital signs are checked every few minutes. It is where I should have been most safe and cared for. In a general ward there is less capacity for such dedicated observation. So, what happened that had me screaming in agony?

Over the next few days I was able to pull some of the pieces together. I discovered that ICUs are managed a little differently to other wards in that the chain of command is independent to whatever surgeons or anaesthetists may advise. Ultimately, it is the ICU doctor who decides on the level of analgesia administered to a patient. It means that ICU functions as an insular body. Still, this didn't exactly explain what went wrong in my instance. I wanted answers. I asked to see the head of ICU for an explanation and an apology.

In the meantime, I attempted to continue writing Alice's story on my laptop from the hospital bed. Of course, I achieved little but the attempt grounded me and held me to something beyond my immediate circumstance. Even looking at photos of Alice and her garage girls reminded me life was not just about me and my body. 1920s Melbourne was where I often escaped to when my own reality felt too difficult and it was always propelled by Alice as if I were riding sidecar to her every setback and success. Alice had been able to physically achieve things I never could but my capacity to write and bear witness to her life made us a good team.

It's difficult to self-advocate when healing from such dramatic surgery while being so physically and emotionally vulnerable. Even though I'd asked to see the head of ICU, it was one low ranking ICU staff member after another who came to see me. They commiserated but couldn't give me the information I wanted. I insisted on seeing the head honcho and eventually he was summoned. He acknowledged my suffering and apologised verbally but nothing happened except a lot of nodding and head shaking. End of! The only information I received from him was that I had been in ICU for three to four hours. Knowing I had awoken from the anaesthetic not long after being wheeled in, this meant I had suffered excruciating pain for at least three hours. No wonder I'd gone bonkers.

The medical notes made at the time in no way did justice to what I'd actually experienced. I think the descriptive word was 'discomfort'. But perhaps I was so out of it I'd been deluded. Patients can be easily dismissed as having a poor perception of their own reality. The only witnesses to my 'discomfort' were the ICU staff and any other poor sod of a patient who had to endure my screams. I felt like I was being reduced to that four-year-old who knew the nurse was wrong to give me medicine and a piece of chocolate before surgery but with no recourse except to suffer the consequences of her mistake.

Once out of hospital I spoke to a friend who had recently retired as an ICU nurse. She'd worked in a different hospital and I'd never been her patient but what she suggested to me was shocking and made sense. One: I'd arrived in ICU on a Friday night when it's not so easy to contact relevant specialists for advice. Two: Having been a patient for so many years my medical files are huge and not easy to navigate, so perhaps some information wasn't read or was missing. And, most importantly, three: ICU doctors often decide on the amount of analgesia a patient receives based on their size and weight. That there, for me, was the clincher. I am small. At my heaviest I weigh around fifty-five kilos. But, as we know, the more analgesia one takes over time the more one needs. I had been on necessarily high doses of pain relief for months.

The post-operative analgesia administered to me was a drug called Ketamine. It's a general anaesthetic that is also used to numb pain when conscious. And, alarmingly, it's a party drug of choice for some due to its dissociative and hallucinogenic effects. As one source states, 'It distorts perceptions of sight and sound and makes the user feel disconnected and not in control ... Ketamine can produce a state of sedation, immobility, relief from pain, and amnesia.' Clearly it is not something you'd want to have too much of. An overdose could be fatal just like the anaesthetic, Propofol, that killed Michael Jackson. The ICU doctors were wise to be cautious, but it appears they didn't put their concerns in context when it came to my situation. I came to discover that they had allegedly HALVED my recommended Ketamine dose!

I eventually recovered, following yet another post-operative infection and the subsequent adjustments required when a spine can no longer move. The pay-off is my pain is greatly reduced, especially in my lower back. However, it is far from a normal-looking spine. Despite this, I have gained approximately three centimetres in height. When I asked my surgeon why the shape was not as natural as I'd hoped he said he had no choice. It was a decision based on a complicated mathematical equation. Had he not followed this equation I would have been left permanently leaning forward. He did the best with what he had and I thank him for it.

A few years after the surgery I cobbled the strength to write a letter of complaint to the hospital. I couldn't bring myself to attempt it any sooner due to symptoms suggestive of Post Traumatic Stress Disorder. PTSD diagnosis and treatment is expensive, not always helpful and not something I can afford to pursue. However, PTSD is often caused by accumulated trauma. I'm often hyper-vigilant and sometimes have recurring night-mares involving torture and entrapment but overall, on a daily basis, I cope.

I do believe I haven't been as negatively affected as I could otherwise have been by such traumatic events. I'm not sure why, but I seem to have developed a technique of 'forgetting' the trauma of severe physical pain, perhaps not unlike a woman who forgets the trauma of childbirth as a survival mechanism. The fact that I was born into this situation has also more than likely inured me to the more shocking effects of acquired pain and disability experienced by those unused to such experiences. Still, one cannot live through such things and not be left without emotional and psychological scars.

Back to my letter of complaint. What was the point? What outcome did I expect? I made it clear that I was absolutely not interested in legal action. I couldn't see how that would do me any favours when I had no choice but to continue to rely on the very medical system that had caused me harm. What I wanted was a meeting of hospital stakeholders to address what had happened and to find solutions so that no other patient had to experience what I'd gone through. I wanted it to be a catalyst for cultural change.

A few weeks after I sent off the letter I got a reply. It stated that all the ICU staff, including the manager, had since moved on and there was nothing further that could be done. Full stop! Letter filed! End of! Was I disappointed? Yes! Surprised? No!

## Other lands—six: the bucket-list trip

2018, a year after my spinal fusion, was a bucket-list trip. I persuaded Carolyn to accompany me to South America and on a cruise to Antarctica. I wanted to see those amazing cliffs of blue-white ice before they melted into our warming oceans.

But our trip didn't quite go to plan. An unexpected 'weather event' in Sydney had us missing our connecting flights and the travel package arranged by a company that should have known better, left no wiggle room between that flight and the ship's departure from Buenos Aires. The compromise was extra time in Argentina and Chile. It was disappointing but feedback from a tourist we met who had been on the Antarctic cruise was horrific enough for me to be grateful we were spared. According to her, the experience of sailing through the Drake Passage was horrendous. Known as the 'Drake Shake', the gateway to Antarctica had unusually violent waves rising ten metres or more. The ship roiled so much most passengers vomited rather than ate. And there was an unseasonal snowstorm. A few hardy travellers who insisted on taking Zodiac dinghies to stay overnight on one of the icebergs had their folly exposed when one of the men sank so far into the ice and snow he fractured his knee cap. Had I been on the trip I wouldn't have ventured off the ship in that sort of weather but I still have nightmares about those enormous waves. The increasing effects of climate change had urged me to the base of the world but it was climate change that prevented me from getting there.

As well as packing elbow crutches I'd hired an electric scooter for the trip. The scooter was the only way I could travel longer walking distances and it was so freeing after dragging myself around on crutches most of the time. The downside to needing an electric chair was the uneven ground I often had to traverse and the fear of running out of battery power. But I managed to wheel around the outdoor markets in Santiago and take in the beautiful 1930s architecture in Buenos Aires. I lost count of how many elaborate doorways I photographed in that city. Those portals were works of art. Wandering around Argentina's capital, we also came across a women's rights rally fighting for liberation. We could not speak their language but the messages were the same as in any country fighting for such things. Close by, there was a public park housing a number of brightly painted wooden kennels for homeless pooches. They reminded me of the colourful beach boxes back home. Chained to each kennel was a water bowl and we were told volunteers ensured the bowls were always filled.

In Peru, I took in the ruins of Machu Picchu, the fifteenth century citadel seated high in the Andes Mountains. I ventured on elbow crutches along the shortest route and eventually found a wooden bench under a thatched roof where I could sit and observe. It was drizzling and the sun flashed back and forth among sweeping clouds that exposed then obliterated the crumbling stone dwellings. I watched as a girl of about ten jerked past with a walking frame. She appeared to have cerebral palsy and had an adult walking either side of the frame, carefully assisting her over the more difficult terrain. Her uphill progress prompted me to move from the bench and see what other vantage points I could find despite the drizzle. While Carolyn and other tourists traipsed up and down with phones and cameras in front of their faces, I took in the solitude, the gentle winds, the sun and the passing clouds.

In the Galapagos Islands, I lounged on volcanic rocks surrounded by marine iguanas while others scuba-dived off boats and climbed extinct volcanoes. Carolyn returned exhausted and disappointed each time. The tour guides apparently left the scuba divers flailing in the water for at least two hours and the arduous climb up the volcano revealed the wonder at its pinnacle as a dry scoop of earth covered in scraggly grass. They didn't once come across any of the promised wildlife. Meanwhile, I wandered, on my crutches, through waters of dancing flamingoes and beaches of resting seals. I bought a genuine handmade Panama hat to keep off the sun and drank milk from freshly picked coconuts. I couldn't physically do everything the other tourists managed but much of my experience felt like a sacred meditation.

## What would Alice do?

2018. The historical importance of Alice and her innovative garage service continued to capture the public imagination. Apart from my ongoing Facebook blogging and calls from film and TV producers, I'd consulted with curators the year prior and appeared as guest at the launch of the Alice Anderson exhibition at the National Motor Museum in Birdwood, South Australia. The semi-permanent exhibition recreated Alice's garage in detail, including written information, photographs and interactive displays.

But what of her biography that I'd struggled so long to pull together? What I'd been doing—getting feedback from my writing group, polishing the manuscript, sending it off to publishers—had so far been for nought, even with increasing interest in Alice. I could have chosen to self-publish but, being my first serious attempt at getting a book out, I wasn't confident enough to do this without a traditional publisher confirming my manuscript justified Alice's life story. Instinct told me I had only one shot at this and the story, which I understood to be such an important contribution to Australian history (and specifically lesbian history), that it needed to be acknowledged and supported beyond a self-published platform. I was a nobody and I didn't want Alice sinking back into historical oblivion along with her 'author'.

It is the twin task of any serious writer to at once be comfortable with long periods of concentrated focus as well as outwardly promoting the work once it's completed—to become an extrovert after a sustained period of introversion. If I was going to give this manuscript wings, I needed to step away from the comfort of my computer and rustle up some serious support. I took a breath and asked myself what would Alice do? One: she wouldn't take 'No!' for an answer. Two: she'd think outside the box. Three: she'd take an entrepreneurial approach.

I began contacting literary agents but soon realised it was even more difficult to secure an agent than a publisher. In the increasingly cutthroat world of traditional publishing few agents or publishers were prepared to take a commercial risk with a relatively unknown writer. Credibility meant having an agent, a book already published, a publisher already interested.

What did Alice do to break into the motor garage business? She made contacts, she networked with people of influence. She 'worked the room'. I swallowed my discomfort and did the same. Who could I approach with enough of a profile who'd be generous enough to read a couple of my chapters and give me an endorsement?

I contacted several people: a well-known lesbian actor of stage and screen; a lesbian historian specialising in women and motoring; a male historian specialising in Australian history; a female historian specialising in Australian history and a much beloved author whose recurring character solves crimes in 1920s Melbourne. All agreed to read three chapters from the manuscript and I chose different chapters for each, depending on their background and interests. All gave me genuinely positive feedback and I am forever grateful to them.

Armed with these endorsements I again applied to publishers and agents. Where the space for 'publishing history' had blinked back at me with a huge question mark I now broke the rules and instead listed my endorsements under the heading 'praise for the manuscript'. Then I sat back and waited.

Months went by until a crack of light came through. As it turned out, the endorsements I had collected led to the biggest endorsement of all—a literary agent who believed the manuscript had legs and went in to bat for me. Jacinta di Mase of JDM literary management made contact and agreed to read the full manuscript. More months of waiting and then I was told several publishers were interested. A bidding war eventually broke out between three publishers, one of whom had rejected the manuscript when I had originally submitted it sans agent. The door was now wide open. Suddenly Alice and I were driving full speed ahead. I held tight, suspecting it was she who had full control of the vehicle and I was just along for the ride.

There were decisions to make, contracts to sign, and editors to deal with. The process from contract to publication, which could have taken up to two years, suddenly became a six-month proposition after I mentioned that the hundred-year anniversary of the opening of Alice's Kew Garage would be in 2019. I was now on an exciting, nail-biting and exhausting race to get things finalised in time. Suddenly there were two editors assigned to polish the manuscript. It was like being back at school with teachers correcting my assignments with red pen and comments in the margins. Every fact had to be double-checked, every sentence, paragraph, chapter polished over and over. It was a rude awakening and confirmation that, however objective a writer believes they are about their own work, an experienced editor can always see where improvements can be made. I worked diligently, so captured in the process that I spent days in my dressing gown forgetting to take meal breaks. At one point I sat amongst a shower of my own shedding skin—a negative reaction to a new medication I'd been given for bone density. Layers of skin cells literally flaked off me as if I were living in my own special snow dome. Just as well I had an excuse not to leave the house. The book, *A Spanner in the Works: The extraordinary story of Alice Anderson and Australia's first all-girl garage* was finally released by Hachette in April 2019.

I set up the book launch, along with a photographic exhibition, at the Hawthorn Arts Centre, just a few blocks from where Alice lived and worked, and where she had been laid to rest in Boroondara (Kew) Cemetery. Friends, family, relatives of Alice and the garage girls, as well as the general public poured through the doors. The dress theme was 1920s and I'd arranged prizes for 'best costume' for which my mother, erstwhile dressmaker and lover of fashion, was judge and jury. I wore a beautiful 1920s style outfit Mum had made for herself years ago, which included a felt cloche hat she had specially ordered to match. I finished off my look with 20s-style French leather shoes from an op-shop and a feather boa.

If my job was to re-write Alice into the history books, then I had succeeded. It had taken a decade of patience, innumerable setbacks and much support from many but persistence finally did pay off. Since then, the book has been optioned for a TV drama series and turned into the play, *Garage Girls,* which was performed in a local theatre in Melbourne in 2023. There have been interviews; radio programs; podcasts; newspaper and magazines articles. Offers to present talks on Alice Anderson continue pouring in from libraries, schools, gay and lesbian organisations, car clubs and other community groups. Government financial support for young female entrepreneurs in Victoria has been named The Alice Anderson Fund. Two local Boroondara women have helped to get an historical marker placed near the garage site and the three of us are now working on raising money for an Alice Anderson statue which, if successful, will be the first female statue to be erected in the City of Boroondara.

Alice is still in control of the vehicle. I just go where she leads me. *Qui n'a risqué rien na rien*—Nothing ventured, nothing gained.


## It's all in the scars

Australia's ancient continent is made deep red by its iron and aluminium oxides and white from silicates and salt. It has one of the largest uranium deposits in the world, from which nuclear medicine is used to diagnose and treat patients. The titanium holding my skeleton in a quasi-functional state comes from excavating solidified molten lava. I cannot extricate myself from the earth scarred by monstrous machinery—some so large they can be seen from space.

Many Indigenous peoples have used ritual scarification to denote initiation, status, tribal identity and adornment. Colonisation has largely nullified the practice, but Australian Aboriginal elders remember their importance, not just on the body but on the land. 'The cuttings all over our country are also our people. The cuts are a stamp or a seal' says Bill Yidumduma Harney of the Wardaman Aboriginal Corporation in the Northern Territory, 'These cuts on our bodies relate to the rock paintings. The maburn [tribal marks] on the rock are like a letter that tells people they are in Wardaman tribal land.' As Yidumduma Bill Harney explains, without any cuts you were a 'cleanskin' and you could not trade, marry, or sing ceremonial songs.

The largest cuttings across our land now come from mining corporations who, at times, blast ancient Aboriginal sacred sites into oblivion.

Sacred. An embedded acronym of scar.

It is now a fashion amongst young of any background to visit scarification artists who carve the epidermal layer with a scalpel, a heated brand or an abrasive tool to create patterns on the body. Personal markings within a tribe of individualism. Traditionally, scars were made deliberately more prominent by pressing substances into the wound, such as wood ash or clay, which also served to stop the bleeding. Modern scarification artists use iodine, citrus juice or toothpaste to slow the healing and raise the surface.

All who scarify themselves are inscribing a visible and permanent message, a language, a story on the skin's surface. Even a scarring on the earth's skin cannot be completely covered over. The land always comes back differently.

A scar is produced in the body by a complex cellular and chemical inflammatory response. It contains less elastin and more collagen, which makes the skin tight with less flexibility. Despite my collagen defect my scars are normal. The abnormality sits beneath.

Surgical scars are like tailings pointing to activity below the surface. They leave a memory on the body at the core of each disturbed epidermal layer. They are testament to the violence of disturbance and healing. Few people with a surgical scar would want it to become any more prominent than it needs to be nor would deliberately seek to belong to a surgically scarred tribe of individuals. For most it is a symbol of endurance rather than pride. If I'd had a choice to survive without surgery, I would have remained a cleanskin.

I have seen tattoos designed to camouflage scars. Some are wonderfully artistic. But why would I want symbols carved with inked needles when a scalpel has been at play across so much surface? I would be disguising my original stories with something else, as if a reinterpretation would aesthetically improve something.

My scars on both thighs have been opened and reopened more times than I care to count. The original scar on my left leg, which was crudely carved in the 1960s has since been subsumed by further incisions and, at one point, ironically appeared smaller and neater than the first. That was until the infected metal plate supporting my femur had to be replaced. Now the area is a roadmap of scars. But I can still see the dotting either side from the sewing together with thick waxed cotton and needle from the first time my body met with a scalpel and I lost my cleanskin status. Today, most surgical wounds are stapled so the dots are tiny to non-existent though occasionally a staple escapes retrieval and buries itself.

After my left knee replacement, the long scar on my left thigh extended across my knee and down a few centimetres along my shinbone like a road stopping short of its destination. The visiting nurse and I wondered why a tiny section of my post-operative wound refused to heal.

'Wait!' I said, sensing a glint of metal.

She gently fiddled with her sterile tweezers until we both saw it. Once I knew it was there my urge to have it excised immediately was overwhelming. The staple was one piece of metal that needed to be mined from my flesh.

'Get it out now, please!' I said. She looked at me, questioningly. 'I know it'll hurt but just do it, I'll be okay. Even if I yell out, don't stop.'

She took out a scalpel and began to pull back the skin. I gritted my teeth and growled but reassured her to keep going. She finally prised it out of the bloody hole and the relief was immediate. The scar formed from her excavation that day is an additional story to all the other carvings my body has endured.

The scar on my right leg stops short of my knee but it may well travel further if my right knee ever gets replaced. The top of my right leg scar ends across the side of my right buttock. This is a result of the hip revision attached to the long rod. It aligns with the circular shaped scar against my left hip where, at four years old, wire was fixed to my hip joint and projected into the plaster. It is not quite as circular as it would have been had the nurse not snagged it while attempting to alleviate my itching plaster-covered skin.

The scar to dwarf all others runs from my lower back up to my shoulders. I can feel that it is unusually thick from being re-opened to clean out the post-operative infection, but I have never seen it. People have offered to take photos for me, but I graciously decline. It is the price for much reduced back pain, but I don't need to see that final long, long scar to remind me that the physical results are deep, restrictive and unchangeable. I feel the effects of this surgery every day. I can only bend from my hips. I cannot arch or bend my back, twist or turn my neck as far as I used to. From a state of hyper-flexion I have become stiffened with rods, plates, screws and increasingly, osteoarthritis. Cursed by Medusa and turned to stone, you may say, but not quite petrified.

The deepest scars, of course, are the invisible ones. The cutting of the mind into tentacles of trauma laced through every cell. A constant swill of experience, memory, sense and feeling. It's a feedback loop I attempt to psychologically transmute into something resembling strength, positivity, defiance. Whatever has been done to me and will be done to me in the name of science, ignorance, neglect or intentional harm, I continue to work at protecting my Self. Once the soul, if you will, is lost, the rest disintegrates so we hold on for dear life. This is how we all survive damage, whatever form it takes. We may not resurface in the same way but nobody alive escapes being disabled, disenfranchised or othered in one way or another. As long as we stand in light there is always shadow, always something to challenge truth, justice, knowledge, physical and mental wellbeing. As humans we are at once strong, yet vulnerable, immutable and forever changing.

Bury me and once my flesh is gone my bones will give up their carapace of molten lava. Turn me to ash and I will leave you with a titanium sculpture for my headstone, perfectly polished to reflect the sun. You could leave me there, casting shadows or turn me into aerospace components and have me float among the stars. My scars will no longer matter but it will be enough that I have lived.

# NOTES

## Chapter 2: The Adults Are in Charge

Information on opioid use in children under the sub-heading 'The infancy of infant pain' comes from 'Pain Management in Children' by Dilip Pawar and Lars Garten, a chapter in the book, *Guide to Pain Management in Low-Resource Settings* edited by Andreas Kopf and Nilesh B. Patel and published by the International Association for the Study of Pain in 2010.

For further reading on the use of morphine with children, see 'Morphine and Children: An Australian perspective', by H. A. Kilham, M. Grant and M. Mherekumombe in the *Journal of Paediatrics and Child Health*, Royal Australian College of Physicians, 2015, pp. 482–483.

For more on infantile amnesia, under the sub-heading 'Plastered all the way from Paris', see <https://www.healthline.com/health/why-cant-i-remember-my-childhood> accessed 23 December 2022>. First published 10 February 2021, current version updated 1 February 2023.

## Chapter 5: Taking Control

Further to the education policies mentioned under the sub-heading 'A top-heavy tertiary learning curve', Coalition Prime Minister, Malcolm Fraser, succeeded Gough Whitlam after Whitlam's dismissal in 1975. Fraser's government was known as the 'razor gang' due to its unwinding of many radical social justice reforms introduced by the previous government, including the dismantling of free tertiary education. I was involved in several student protests fighting against the reintroduction of university fees.

**Chapter 7: Descensus**
All Dante quotes cited in this chapter are from *The Divine Comedy: Inferno* by Dante Alighieri, first published in Italy, 1492. I used the English translation by Henry Wadsworth Longfellow, 1867 Published by Project Gutenberg, eBook #1001, first published in digital format, 1 August 1997 and updated 6 April 2021. Quotes as they appear in chronological order in the chapter, including subheading, come from the following passages:

Inferno: Canto XXVII p. 616.
Inferno: Canto VI p. 150.
Inferno: Canto XXIII p. 526.
Inferno: Canto VII p. 154.
Inferno: Canto XXXIII p. 762.
Inferno: Canto II p. 61.
Inferno: Canto I p. 19.
Inferno: Canto XIII p. 294.
Inferno: Canto XXXIV p. 776.
Inferno: Canto II p. 55.

A useful reference on opioids and pain relief measures is 'The challenge of perioperative pain management in opioid-tolerant patients' by Flaminia Coluzzi, Francesca Bifulco, Arturo Cuomo, Mario Dauri, Claudio Leonardi, Rita Maria Melotti, Silvia Natoli, Patrizia Romualdi, Gennaro Savoia & Antonio Corcione and published in 2017 in the journal, *Therapeutics and Clinical Risk Management*, pp. 1163–1173. <DOI: 10.2147/TCRM.S141332>.

## Chapter 9: Navigating Perspective

For more on chronic pain, discussed under the sub-heading 'Walking on shaky ground: I could have given birth to my own hip', see <https://www.ncbi.nlm.nih.gov/pmc/articles/PMC6676152/>, published online 10 May 2019, and <https://www.nih.gov/news-events/nih-research-matters/scientists-find-new-pain-suppression-center-brain>, published 2 June 2020.

## Chapter 10: Adventures with Alice

Under the sub-heading, 'Alice comes to life on a disability pension', I talk of the article by historian Mimi Colligan about Alice Anderson. That piece, 'Alice Anderson: Garage Proprietor', was in *Double Time: Women in Victoria—150 Years,* edited by Marilyn Lake and Farley Kelly and was published by Penguin Australia in 1985. The article on Alice is on pages 305–311.

## Chapter 11: Extremis Eventus

For more on Ketamine and pain relief, see <https://www.dea.gov/sites/default/files/2020-06/Ketamine-2020.pdf>.

For the information on scarification and Indigenous culture, I am indebted to Yidumduma Bill Harney, of the Wardaman Aboriginal Corporation Northern Territory, who has written the article 'Aboriginal Scarification', as quoted on Australian Museum website and updated on 5 December 2018. <https://australian.museum/about/history/exhibitions/body-art/aboriginal-scarification/>.

# ACKNOWLEDGEMENTS

Deep felt thanks to the extraordinary women at Spinifex for taking on this manuscript with such great care and understanding. It has been such a pleasure to work with you. Also a shout out to my writing group, The Cartridge Family, for valuable feedback on the manuscript as it progressed from an idea to something submittable. And finally, heartfelt thanks goes to my dear friend and fellow writer, Kathleen Mary Fallon, who if not for her input this work would have been far less than the sum of its parts. The memoir went through several titles throughout the course of my writing but it was Kathleen who encouraged me to 'own the gravitas!', gave me the death stare and promptly told me I should call it *Corpus in Extremis*. I dared not refuse!

OTHER BOOKS BY SPINIFEX PRESS

## Sandy Jeffs

### Flying with Paper Wings:
### Reflections on Living with Madness
(Updated edition)

*Highly Commended Certificate in the Human Rights Commission's*
*Non-Fiction Award 2010*
*SANE Book of the Year 2010*
*Shortlisted for The Age Book of the Year Award, 2010*

Sandy Jeffs was diagnosed with schizophrenia in 1976, a time when recovery was seen as unlikely. She was in and out of institutional care for 15 years, including at the infamous Larundel Psychiatric Hospital.

Sandy was among the first to start speaking publicly about living with a mental illness, and much of her writing – including eight volumes of poetry – has been about her struggle to live a full life. She is well-known as a community educator, speaking to doctors and psychiatrists, at community health centres, and educational institutions. She has been honoured in the Victorian Honour Roll of Women, Her Place Women's Museum, and with an OAM in 2020.

*Flying with Paper Wings* offers insights into madness – medical, social, personal – as well as disturbing reflections on its causes and its care. It is also a story of how poetry can become a personal saviour in the face of nearly irresistible forces.

Read this exceptional book. It takes you beyond your own narrow terror towards something that might be called insight.
—Helen Elliott, *The Age*

ISBN 9781925950946   ebook available

# Susan Hawthorne

## The Falling Woman

*1992, The Australian's Best Books of the Year*
*1992 Top Twenty Title, Listener Women's Book Festival (NZ)*

A vivid desert odyssey, *The Falling Woman* travels through a haunting landscape of memory, myth and mental maps. Told in three voices – Stella, Estella and Estelle – this is an inspiring story drawn from childhood memories, imagined worlds and the pressing realities of daily life.

*The Falling Woman* charts one woman's journey into the heartland. It is a journey taken across the desert, into the heart of memory, and into the mythic heart, that place to which we return in times of crisis.

This book commands endless reflection, since it opens up the ontological question of being. Hawthorne's book haunts me, it won't let go. On the one hand, it journeys through an unexplored territory of mind that few apart from Dostoyevski dared look into ... Let me first say that this is a perfectly structured piece of writing. Its form should help unravel the threads of signification, but we are not dealing here with the explicit, let alone the assertive, or blatant. The only certainty Hawthorne has is that nature is her cradle.
—Jasna Novakovic, *Australian Women's Book Review*

ISBN 9781876756369   ebook available

# Suniti Namjoshi

## O Sister Swallow: An Elegy for Bharati Namjoshi

In this exquisite memoir, Suniti Namjoshi reflects on the life of her sister Bharati, their overlapping yet disparate lives, their nearness and distance, and what it means to belong and to be valued.

The two sisters love one another and they love birds; but they live on different continents and think in different languages. Is this what sisterhood is really about – to acknowledge difference and still to understand and to care?

This richly textured book with its tender and elegant language is full of both joy and grief. It is a generous yet poignant invitation from the author to us to contemplate our own experiences.

A deeply moving, genre-disrupting, passionate work, studded with gem-like lines, from the pioneering and always surprising Suniti Namjoshi.

—Ruth Vanita, author of *Love's Rite, Memory of Light* and *A Slight Angle*

ISBN 9781922964083    ebook available

## Fiona Place

### Portrait of the Artist's Mother:
### Dignity, Creativity and Disability

A memoir and an examination of the politics of disability. Fiona Place describes the pressure from medical institutions to undergo screening during pregnancy and the traumatic nature and assumptions that a child with Trisomy 21 should not live, even though people with Down syndrome do live rich and productive lives. Fiona's son, Fraser, has become an artist and his prize winning paintings have been exhibited in galleries in Sydney and Canberra. How does a mother get from the grieving silence of the birthing room through the horrified comments of other mothers to the applause at gallery openings?

This is a story of courage, love and commitment to the idea that all people, including those who are 'less than perfect', have a right to be welcomed into this increasingly imperfect world.

Fiona Place is one of our great truth-tellers. There is no other writer like her.
—Amanda Lohrey, award-winning fiction writer

ISBN 9781925581751    ebook available

# Melinda Tankard Reist (Ed.)

## Defiant Birth: Women Who Resist Medical Eugenics
### (New Edition)

The women in this book may be among the last to have babies without the medical stamp of approval.

Today's society demands physical perfection from all and regards medical and scientific technologies as saviours to be embraced whatever the cost. To have a child who has been diagnosed with a disability is deemed not just unnecessary, but careless and even immoral.

*Defiant Birth* tells the courageous stories of women who continued their pregnancies despite intense pressure from doctors, family members and social expectations. These women were told they shouldn't have their babies because of a perceived imperfection in the child, or because their own disabilities do not fit within the parameters of what a mother should be. In the face of silent disapproval and open hostility, they have confronted the stigma of disability and had their children anyway.

This well-documented and compelling account of the pressures faced by women expecting disabled children calls for every child to be welcomed and loved, and deserves to be heeded by a very wide readership.

— Alison Davis, UK disability activist, author of
*From Where I Sit* and founder of No Less Human

ISBN 9781925581911    ebook available

*If you would like to know more about
Spinifex Press, write to us for a free catalogue, visit our
website or email us for further information
on how to subscribe to our monthly newsletter.*

Spinifex Press
PO Box 105
Mission Beach QLD 4852
Australia

www.spinifexpress.com.au
women@spinifexpress.com.au